Di

This book is based on the authors' personal experiences with their Christian faith, offering those experiences as inspirations to readers who are searching for faith, or renewed faith, in their Catholic Christian tradition.

Glenn Harmon is an ordained Deacon in the Roman Catholic Church and his wife, Linda, is a devote Catholic who accompanies her husband on their missions and retreats across the United States and Canada.

Their stories focus on how God's revelations of His goodness and mercy in their lives inspired them to dedicate their lives to spreading the Gospel of Jesus Christ through more than 500 parish missions over more than 20 years, providing faith-filled insights about living a Christian life filled with God's joy, peace, inspiration and comfort.

Dedication

We would like to dedicate this book, first and foremost, to Our Lord and Savior Jesus Christ, who has always been there for us in good times and bad.

Just as the journey of Jesus led Him to the cross and beyond, His unconditional love, mercy and forgiveness has allowed us to embrace our own crosses, believing in faith that a resurrection will follow.

We also dedicate this book to all our family and friends who have stood by us with their prayers and support.

Our thanks also go to Sister Mary Constance Fitzgerald; our son-in-law, Pastor Dan Crowley and our daughter, Christina Crowley for their efforts in participating in the editing of this book.

Also, we wish to deeply thank John and Roberta Wolcott for their hard work and professionalism. Without their efforts, this book would not have been possible. We thank our Lord for bringing them into our lives.

Table of Contents

Introduction

"But to you who hear, I say love your enemies; do good to those who hate you; bless those who curse you; pray for those who mistreat you. To the person who strikes you on one cheek, offer the other one as well, and from the person who takes your cloak, do not withhold even your tunic. Give to everyone who asks of you, and from the one who takes what is yours, do not demand it back." (Luke 6:27-30)

Jesus, you can't be serious!

"If anyone wishes to come after me, he must deny himself and take up his cross daily and follow me. For whoever wishes to save his life will lose it, but whoever loses his life for my sake will save it." (Luke 9:23-24)

Jesus, you can't be serious!

Then, Peter, approaching, asked Him, "Lord, if someone sins against me, how often must I forgive? As many as seven times?" Jesus answered, "I say to you, not seven times but seventy times seven." (Matthew - 18:22)

Jesus, you can't be serious!

Actually, He was dead serious!

Linda and I were married April 4, 1970. She is not only my wife but also my best friend. Linda is a woman who believes that it's in living by faith that we truly gain the promises of Christ. Her life is a testimony of what hope and faith can be for people in need.

We are Christians in the Catholic tradition. We have been blessed with two beautiful daughters, four amazing grandchildren and a terrific faith community with an abundance of friends and neighbors. Our life is great and we love the Lord Jesus and the abundant life He offers.

But, it was not always this way.

From living in the fast lane as a singer, to achieving a vice presidency in a major national corporation, I had been on the top of my world. Not God's world, but mine. My theme song was, "I did it my way."

Through disobedience, I landed where no person would choose to go. I know that I broke at least eight of God's commandments. My lifestyle almost destroyed my marriage, as well as my relationship with

1

my two daughters. It cost me my career and brought shame, pain and heartache to my family and my Church. I was a broken, wounded and humiliated man.

Only our Lord Jesus, through His grace, mercy, unconditional love and forgiveness would restore my life, our marriage and family while taking us on a journey we never thought possible.

As we write this book, we see wars, poverty, homelessness, racial conflict, exploitation and political gridlock. For the most part, we live in a world that has either forgotten, refuses to accept or does not know there is a Savior. His name is Jesus Christ!

It is our prayer that by reading this book you will:

❖ reawaken and strengthen the faith within you;
❖ encourage you to believe in and accept your uniqueness in Christ;
❖ help you experience the healing power and unconditional love of Jesus Christ;
❖ empower you to share your gifts and talents with others and
❖ enable you to fulfill God's will by living the Scriptures.

It is our hope that this book will inspire, encourage and even challenge you to renew your walk with the Lord. It is a message of hope, love, faith and reconciliation that will bring healing and restoration to you and the relationships around you.

We can confidently say that because the messages in the following chapters changed our lives, marriage and family.

What's In Your Junk Drawer?

Allow us to share a practical and common example of what this book is meant to be for you, our reader. If Linda and I had the privilege of coming to your home, we would probably find something that we have in our home - a "junk drawer." Ours is in the kitchen.

A junk drawer is a place where, when you have something and you don't know what to do with it or you don't want to deal with it at the moment, you open the drawer, drop it inside and forget all about it - until you go to put something else in the drawer and there you find all of that stuff that you had hoped would disappear.

2

If your junk drawer is anything like ours, once or twice a year it gets so full we are forced to do something about it.

Linda and I will take the drawer, dump everything out on a table and start going through it. We take all the trash and junk - you know, the stuff we should never have kept in the first place - and throw it away. What we find remaining are all the things we consider valuable and important.

We take all those things and put them right back in the drawer and start the process all over again.

This book is about cleaning out and rearranging our personal and spiritual junk drawers. It's about taking all the stuff that we carry around with us each day that prevents us from experiencing the abundant life that Jesus promises and getting rid of it.

And, when we do, what is remaining are all the treasures that were buried below all that junk - God's peace, hope, healing, love, joy, faith and forgiveness.

Our ministry begins

Since July of 1992, Linda and I have dedicated our lives to full-time ministry. By faith, we are following a special call from our Lord to share the love of Jesus Christ. For over two decades we have been in ministry, giving over 500 Catholic parish retreats, workshops, seminars and conferences around the United States and Canada.

We do not offer hell fire and brimstone, but rather God's unconditional love as revealed to us in Jesus Christ. We invite people to a greater personal reform and holiness of life, which will then contribute to the strengthening of our marriages, families, Church and society.

We chose to take to heart and live out the words of Jesus in the Gospel of Matthew 28: 19-20.

"Go, therefore, and make disciples of all nations, teaching them to observe all that I have commanded you. And, behold, I am with you always, until the end of the age."

This Gospel is referred to by theologians and Scripture scholars as the Great Commission. In essence, it is the final marching order of Jesus to His apostles. I can just imagine their reactions. "Really Lord! You can't expect us to go out and save the world. We're just ordinary people and fishermen."

Up to this point, the apostles had been eye witnesses, simply observers. But now Jesus was calling them to witness to Christ's teachings by being living examples of those teachings.

He was offering them three things:

1) a purpose greater than themselves,
2) the assurance of His power, and
3) a promise that He would always be with them.

Linda and I have experienced all of these promises two thousand years later in our lives and ministry.

None of the apostles could have imagined how far their "yes" to Jesus would take them or how much fruit they would bear for His Kingdom. Jesus made it so the people they encountered would accept Him as Lord not on the basis of their ability or preaching skills but in response to His own grace working in their hearts.

Christ's ministry inspires us

But these words were not only meant for 12 men on a mountain. Christianity for 2000-plus years has flourished because other people just like you and me have taken the words of Jesus seriously. Each of us has been created for a mission. Our English word "mission" comes from the Latin word for "sending."

Jesus clearly understood His mission on Earth. At 12 years old, He said, "I must be about my Father's work." Twenty-one years later, while hanging on the cross He said, "It is finished."

While we are on this Earth, I believe we have some key purposes.

1) to accept Jesus as Lord and Savior.
2) to be a part of His family.
3) to become more like Him.
4) to serve Him.
5) to love Him.

Nothing else we will ever do matters as much as helping people establish an earthly and eternal relationship with Jesus Christ. Your mission, my mission, is so important that Jesus repeated it five times in five different ways in five different books of the Bible. It's as if He was - and is - saying, "I really want you to get this."

If your friend or neighbor had a life threatening illness and you knew the cure, it would be sinful to withhold that life saving information. However, it would be ultimately more damaging to keep secret the true way to love, forgiveness, mercy, peace and eternal life.

We have the greatest news in the world. We have a Savior and His name is Jesus Christ. Our mission and purpose has eternal consequences. Fulfilling your mission does not mean that you have to do what Linda and I do. God wants you to share the Good News of Jesus in your daily life - as parents, as grandparents, as children, where you work, where you go to school and in your neighborhood.

So what is the cost?

It requires that we surrender our agenda and accept God's purpose and plan for our life.

But here is the Good News.

If we will commit to fulfilling our mission in life, no matter what the cost, we will experience the blessings of God in ways that few people ever experience.

Over 20 years ago, Linda and I were giving a Catholic parish retreat in Louisiana. As usual, I was preaching at all the weekend Masses before the retreat started.

I'll always remember Percy

After one of the Masses, I was outside the church visiting and saying goodbye to people as they were leaving to go home. That morning, I met a man I will never forget.

He told me his name was Percy, that he was 63 years old and had been a Catholic all of his life. He then went on to tell me that he had never gone to a parish retreat, but he was planning on coming to this one.

As you can imagine, his comment peaked my interest.

I said, "Percy, why have you made the choice to never go to a parish retreat but you're making the decision to attend this one?"

I noticed that tears started to well up in his eyes.

"Six months ago my wife died," he said. "Over those six months I have realized that I have a hole inside of me. No matter what I try to do, I just can't fill it up. I am hoping that you might say something, or God will do something, to at least begin to fill up the hole."

I wished him a blessed retreat.

After the third night of the retreat, I was in the front pew spending some quiet time in prayer. I felt a hand on my shoulder and when I looked up I saw it was Percy. He said, "Glenn, I don't know if you remember me, but I am the man who told you over the weekend that I had a hole inside of me."

I told him I certainly remembered him.

He said, "I can't completely explain this, and I know that I will never be able to adequately understand, but tonight as I was sitting in my pew simply listening, somehow God completely filled up that hole I had inside and He made it very clear that if I will just let Him, He will keep it filled everyday."

I believe that for many different reasons and circumstances, we are all just like Percy. We have a hole inside of us. I call it a God hole. We spend our lives running around trying to fill it up with everything BUT God. Our Lord wants to fill up the hole in your life.

It is Linda's and my hope that you will not only read the words in this book but, like Percy, listen to them with what St. Benedict calls the "ear of your heart."

May our Lord bless you on your journey of faith.

Deacon Glenn Harmon
and Linda Harmon

Chapter 1

Roadblocks to Victory

For over a decade, God has been nudging us to write a book sharing the messages He has given us to preach and teach.

Over the past 22 years, countless numbers of people have been asking us to put our spoken words into written form.

My wife Linda was willing and eager to begin this project years ago, but I have been dragging my feet.

Why?

Because it would force me to confront my two greatest roadblocks, fear of rejection - fear that nobody would want to read anything we have to say and rejection because if they did read the book it would be looked upon as a failure.

Thousands of saints, theologians, Scripture scholars and academics have written books on God, Church and various aspects of spirituality.

What else could we say that has not already been explored and said?

However, God has not stopped nudging and people continue to ask, so I will attempt with God's grace to overcome my roadblocks and be obedient to God. This book is not supposed to be a theological symposium or a doctrinal dissertation. Linda and I are very simple and ordinary people. We have written this book just like we talk, in a very simple manner.

I want you to know that Linda and I thank God for each and every one of you reading this book, because, like the people we've met at more than 500 parish missions, workshops and retreats in the United States and Canada since 1992, we believe you've felt the need to take time to deepen and strengthen your relationship with almighty God.

We believe that's why you're reading this book. If you didn't want to have a better understanding of God and a better relationship with Him, you would be reading something else.

Also, we believe with everything in us, that God is going to honor your faithfulness.

We also want you to realize that you're not reading this by accident.

The Holy Spirit has been prompting you, nudging you, and you have responded to His prompting.

One of the joys, one of the great pleasures, that Linda and I receive as we travel the country is that we have an opportunity to meet family that we didn't realize we had. I'm speaking about you.

You see, if we can come to an agreement that we all come from one God, God the Father, and that Jesus Christ is our Lord, Savior, and Brother, then in the eyes of God we are family. Over the years, Linda and I have found it doesn't make any difference what city or state we're in, there are several things that never change.

We've discovered that when people such as yourself will take the time and make the sacrifice necessary to come to a mission, or read a book like this, you are generally in one of three places in your spiritual life. We think each and every one of you will be able to relate to one of these spiritual areas.

Some of you are in what I call a resurrection moment in your life. Everything is going great for you. You just want to wrap yourselves in it because it feels good. You're reading this because you're aware of that and you want to know how you can continue to be in that resurrection moment.

Secondly, some of you are reading this because you know there's something missing in your life. You may not even know what it is. But you know there's a void, you know there's a hole. You hope that by reading this book, God will not only make you aware of what is missing but God will help fill up that void, that hole that you sense is within you.

And some of you are reading this because of something that happened in your past or something that's going on in your life right at this very moment.

You're broken, you're wounded, you're hurting and you're in need of the healing touch of God.

I want you to remember that Jesus is the divine healer, the supreme physician who knows exactly what you need. If you read this with an open mind and an open heart, willing and eager to receive whatever God has in store for you, we believe that your life will change for the better.

Three vital questions for you to answer

I'd like to start by asking you three questions. I caution you not to answer these questions too quickly. Your answers are just between you and God. And since God knows the answers to these questions you might as well be as honest as you possibly can.

These are key questions that people have been struggling with for 2,000 years and people will continue to struggle with these questions until God calls us home.

Question number one:

Do you believe that Jesus Christ is really who he says he is?

Question number two:

Do you believe that the promises of Jesus are true?

And, question number three:

Do you believe the promises of Jesus are for you?

Now, look at how you honestly answered those questions at this moment in your life - not how you want them to be or how you hope they might be in the future - but, how you honestly answered them right now. Your answers to those questions are dramatically affecting the choices you're making in your life and how you're living your life.

Over 20 years ago, a very spiritual and wise man asked me those same questions. Without even thinking I answered "yes" to all of them.

Yes, I believed that Jesus Christ is really who he says he is; yes, I believed that the promises of Jesus are true, and yes, I believed the promises of Jesus are for me.

Maybe that's how you've just answered those questions, too - without even thinking.

Well, God knows each of us better than that.

Despite my confident answers, within about a week, in various ways, as only God can, He began to show me the areas of my life that He knew I refused to surrender, areas of my life that I wouldn't let go of, areas of my life where I wanted to hang onto control.

9

I realized the things He was showing me were reminders that there were areas of my life that I did not surrender because in those areas of my life I did not believe He was who He said He was.

Because if I had believed that, I would have freely given Him those areas of my life that I had held back.

Of course, He was right.

At that point in my life, I had given God a lot. But there were certain things that I had not truly surrendered to him, just in case Jesus wasn't who he said he was, just in case Jesus couldn't or wouldn't come through. I kept a little bit back. I held on to some things.

You see our whole life should be about surrender. Our whole life should be about giving up. But, we live in a world, in a society, that promotes "grab it, keep it and, when you have it, don't ever let it go."

The Gospel of Jesus is about exactly the opposite. It's all about giving up, surrendering, giving in and letting go.

So I'm asking you as you begin this book, what areas of your life are you still holding on to, what areas of your life are you refusing to let go of and give to God?

Maybe it's a marriage that's not working as you want it to work. You've been doing everything you can to fix that marriage and it's still not getting fixed. You're holding on to it so tightly. Why don't you surrender it, let it go, give it to God and allow God to fix it?

Maybe it's children who are doing and saying things you never, ever thought they would do or say. You have exhausted every possibility, you have done everything you can possibly think of to fix those kids and they're not being fixed. And, you're holding on to them so tight that you're smothering the relationship. Let go of them and give them to God, who created them in the first place.

We create barriers between us and God

Our Catholic church teaches us that 2,000 years ago, when Jesus went to the cross, that single act re-connected and re-established the broken relationship between humanity, which we are all part of, and God our Father.

If, in fact, that is true - and it is - why is it that so often we believe there is this big wall between us and God, that there are all these roadblocks, all these obstacles that make it so difficult for us to get close to God?

Very simply, when Jesus went to the cross, he moved all these roadblocks, obstacles and barriers out of our way. Yet, everyday we put them right back.

When Jesus moves them out of the way again, we put them back again.

Now, I don't think there are any of us who wake up in the morning and deliberately say, "Today, I'm going to put as many roadblocks between me and God as possible."

But, because of our weakness, our humanness and our sinfulness we put up all of these obstacles that prevent us from having the deeply intimate personal relationship with God that we all want.

You know, our spiritual journey is like any other journey we go on. First, our journey starts at the moment of conception. I'm speaking about our spiritual journey here on earth. It starts at our conception and it goes on until God calls us home.

It's like all other journeys that we take. There are certain things that we want to take with us, things that will improve and benefit our journey. But, there are also things that we want to leave behind, things that will weight us down, things that will prevent us from truly experiencing the beauty of our journey.

If you look at this book as your guide on your journey, as a pilgrimage, I think it's very appropriate that we look at what I call spiritual roadblocks. These are things that prevent us from being the people that God wants us to be.

As this chapter unfolds, I'm going to tell you about six spiritual roadblocks, things that prevent us from doing the things that God wants us to do, things that would bring us closer to God.

It's helpful to remember that the first step toward making any kind of change is awareness. You cannot change anything in your life until you become aware of what needs to be changed.

Before we examine the nature of these roadblocks, I want you to be aware that the only reason I can discuss these spiritual roadblocks is because either I have dealt with each of these, in one way or another, or I am still dealing with them. Let me assure you that you're not alone in your struggles.

I believe that every one of us is struggling with at least one of these spiritual roadblocks. Until we become aware of them, and until we can do something about them, we will never be the person that God wants us to be, which I believe is also the kind of person each of us really wants to be.

I'm talking about those spiritual roadblocks that rob us of our peace of mind and soul. That's why I call the first two roadblocks spiritual thieves, spiritual robbers. What do they steal, what do they rob? They rob our peace of mind and soul, our hope for the future and our joy of the moment.

Every one of us wants peace. I can't imagine anybody reading this who's thinking, "Jesus, keep your peace, I just want more stress and anxiety."

We all have more stress and more anxiety than we can possibly deal with. Yet, we all want to have that peace Jesus promised that goes beyond all understanding. Are you willing to do what is necessary to gain that peace? Recognizing these roadblocks to victory, and how to remove them, can make all the difference in finding God's peace in your life.

The past and the future

Now, the first roadblock has to do with the past. And, the second roadblock has to do with the future. Together, they rob you of the peace, joy and hope of the present moment. The first one is regret, shame and guilt of the past.

As we travel across North America, we meet so many people who in one way or another, at least in one area of their life, are stuck in the past. Something happened in their past and they are filled with great shame and guilt. And, they will not let it go.

And because they will not let go of the past, they're missing out on so much joy, peace and hope of the present moment.

Is there anything that has happened to you, that still has you stuck in the past? I know that intellectually you realize you cannot change the past. None of us can go back into the past and change anything. What has happened has happened. We can learn from it but we can't change it.

However, if there is any regret, shame or guilt about anything that has happened in the past, please surrender that to our Lord before you read on.

He stands ready to take that regret, shame or guilt from the past and he'll heal you of that and pour out his abundant peace, hope and joy to change your life.

Later in this chapter, I will give you a 5-step process to surrendering anything to God.

Now, the second spiritual roadblock has to do with the future. It's called fear.

Once again, I want to tell you that during the more than 500 missions, retreats and spiritual presentations Linda and I have presented since 1992, we have meet so many people who are literally paralyzed with fear about something that might happen.

It hasn't happened yet. And, it may never happen.

But because it might, they're filled with fear.

Now, there's something important to understand about fear.

Fear does not start out as fear.

Fear starts out as concern. I'm concerned about something. Now, if you don't get a handle on that concern, that concern will turn into worry. Now, I'm worried about something. And, if you don't get a handle on that worry, I can promise you, that worry will turn into full-blown, paralyzing fear.

Let me give you an example.

At one of our parish missions Linda and I were giving, this lady came up to me afterward. I guess I've been doing these missions long enough now that I just got this really strong sense she was filled with fear.

I looked at her and I said, "Pardon me, but what are you afraid of?"

She looked at me like I could read her mind.

"Cancer," she said.

"Well, I'm sorry you have cancer."

"No," she said. "I don't."

"OK, some one of your family members has cancer?"

"No," she said.

"So, a friend has cancer?"

"No," she said.

"Well, let me ask you, does anybody you know have cancer?"

"No," she said.

Then, I asked her what she was afraid of.

"I read an article about cancer and I thought what if I get it?" she said. "I am so afraid that I might get it some day."

So you see, there was no evidence of any kind that this beautiful woman was ever going to get cancer. But, because she thought that some day she might get it she was filled with, and consumed by, a paralyzing fear. It was robbing her of every bit of peace, hope and joy in her life. You could look at this woman's face and see that she had no joy, she had no peace.

My brothers and sisters, if anything in your life right now or anything to do with the future, is causing you to be consumed with fear, once again I ask you, invite you, to let it go.

God was very specific when it came to fear. In Isaiah, Chapter 43, verse 1. God said, "Fear not."

Isn't that just like God? God doesn't say, "OK, you can be afraid on Monday, Wednesday and Friday, but on the other days, just don't do it.

God simply says, "Fear not."

God knew that if we were filled with fear it would stop us, prevent us, keep us from being the people that he wants us to be.

If there is anything in your life right now that you're afraid of, surrender and give it to God. He will heal you and set you free.

Your responsibility is to surrender. Let it go. Partnership with God! He will set you free and he will fill you with his abundant peace, hope and love.

Those are the first two spiritual roadblocks - regret, guilt and shame about the past and fear of the future.

Choosing to believe
what others say about you

Now we come to the third roadblock and I have to tell you up front, this one seems to be the most difficult roadblock for people. I have seen it over and over again.

This third roadblock is choosing to believe what other people say about you rather than what God says about you.

This is critical. And the focus word is choosing. Choosing to believe what other people say about you rather than what God says about you.

In just a minute I will tell you exactly what God says about you and exactly what God thinks of you.

But first, let me tell you some of the things that people have told me other people have said to them, things that absolutely destroyed their lives - but only because they chose to believe those things.

And they often believed these things that were said about them because they were generally said to them by people who supposedly loved them and cared for them.

Things such as you're too tall, you're too short, you're fat, you're thin, you're ugly, you're worthless, you're stupid, you're a failure, you shouldn't even bother to try because you will never amount to anything.

Now if we begin to hear those things often enough, over and over and over again, we begin to take it in. We begin to internalize it and we begin to believe it.

I know for certain there are people reading this book, like many of those who come to our missions in churches across the United States and Canada, who have had people say those things about them and it has literally stopped them from becoming the people that God wants them to be.

Now, you may be wondering what God says about each and everyone of us. So, I'm going to tell you. With your Bible still open to Isaiah 43, read down to Verse 4. I want you to realize this is God, your creator, speaking, the God who created and formed you. This is what God says about you.

"You are precious and glorious in my sight and I love you."

That is so powerful that I want to repeat it.

"You are precious and glorious in my sight and I love you."

Right now, as you read this, do you honestly feel precious and glorious in the sight of God?

And, do you believe in the depth of your heart that God loves you?

You see, for far too many years, I thought what God said about being precious and glorious in his sight was meant for everybody else except me. Because when I looked back in my life, and saw so many wrong things that I had done, I wondered how could God possibly say that I am precious and glorious in His sight ... and that He loves me.

That's why I know there are people reading this book, like those attending the hundreds of missions Linda and I have given for the past 20 years, who are saying, "Oh, no. Not me."

There are many other people reading this book who have never even heard those words.

Nobody has ever told them, "God said that you are precious and glorious " and that God loves them. Sadly, there might even be somebody reading this who has never even heard anyone tell them that they are loved, even by the people they truly would love to hear it from.

So, if you're one of those people, how can you believe that a God you cannot see thinks that you are precious and glorious when we never seem to hear, feel or experience those feelings from people who are close to you?

It was about 30 years ago when I realized how important this roadblock is and how devastating it can be in people's lives.

As the director of youth ministry for a Catholic diocese in the United States I did many high school retreats a year. And, at every high school retreat, at some point in that retreat, I would give each one of these teenagers a blank piece of paper and a pencil and tell them to draw a straight vertical line in the center of that paper.

On one side of the line I would ask them to write all the things they don't like about themselves and on the other side I would ask them to list all their different talents, all the special qualities that they believe they have.

And, I never told them which side of the paper to start on.

Ninety-nine percent of those kids would first list everything they didn't like about themselves, every thing that they considered to be wrong. And they had no trouble filling up that whole side of their page.

Why?

Because most of their lives they have heard over and over again, "This is what's wrong with you."

Maybe, if any of those kids came from a home where their parents, their grandparents or whoever was raising them helped them to discover their gifts and talents and positive things about themselves then, maybe, they could write four or five things that they liked about themselves.

I'll never forget one particular retreat. I had just asked the teenagers to do this exercise and I noticed this young lady in the back of the room. I came to find out later that she was a senior in high school.

I saw her fill up one side of the page, which happened to be the side of the paper where she listed everything she didn't like about herself. It only took her about two minutes to do it. Because she had internalized every bit of that negativity, she was carrying it all around within her.

But, as she was starting on the other side of the paper, the positive side, she couldn't think of anything to write down.

I went up to her and asked, "What's the problem?"

She began to cry.

"Mr. Harmon," she said, through her tears, "I have no gifts and talents."

What a tragedy! To be a senior in high school, about ready to go out into the world to make your mark and you honestly believe in the depth of your mind and your heart that you have nothing to give to yourself, to your parents or to anybody else.

Later, while doing adult retreats, I took that same exercise and moved it over to the adults. Guess what, the same thing. You see we live in a world, we grow up in a society, that does not affirm us. We live in a world that says if you look a certain way, talk a certain way, act a certain way, dress a certain way, you're OK, and we love you.

If you don't, we want nothing to do with you. There are people reading this book who honestly believe they have nothing to give to anyone.

17

If you don't gain another thing out of this book, I want you to begin to take into your mind and into your heart that you are precious and glorious in the sight of God, that each and every one of you is a unique, original one-of-a-kind masterpiece of God.

I want to make one more point on that, because if you do not get past this third spiritual roadblock I promise you that you will never, ever become the person that God wants you to be.

I grew up in San Diego, Calif., and spent most of my life there. San Diego is like any other big city. It has very distinctive and beautiful art galleries. Personally, I am not much into art. But I'll never forget this one particular weekend.

One of the six famous art galleries in San Diego was having a one-of-a-kind showing. It had 10 masterpieces on display for one weekend. There were people wrapped around the block, waiting in line for three hours to see these paintings. And they were paying a lot of money to see them.

A newspaper columnist came up to them and asked people in line, "Why are you waiting in line for three hours and spending all of this money to see these paintings?" And every person would say, "Because there's only one like it! If I don't see it now I will never see it again."

I want you to think of yourself and then think of all of the billions and billions of people that God has created before he created you. And think of all of the billions of people that God has created since and all of the people that God has yet to create.

Yet, He created only one of you.

There has never been, there is not now and there never will be another person exactly like you. That makes you more rare than any painting. That makes you more different than any symphony.

If we could truly understand that about one another we'd stand in line just to say "Hi" to each other, because we would begin to realize the kind of a masterpiece each and every one of us is.

Please, realize that you are precious and glorious in the sight of God, because you are, which is why He loves you so much. Still, we put roadblocks into our lives that keep us from the victory God wants us to have.

Understanding your true identity

So far, we've talked about roadblocks that include regret, shame and guilt of the past, fear of the future and choosing to believe what other people say about you rather than what God says about you.

And now we come to the fourth roadblock to victory - understanding your true identity.

Because we don't understand our true identity, the identity that Jesus Christ and our Catholic Church give us, we don't understand that quite often our priorities become misplaced.

We tend to live our lives, to prioritize our lives, based on who we think we are. And, quite often - in fact, if you would allow me to say this, MOST of the time - we have a misunderstanding of who we are and what our true identity is.

That's why I want to tell you who Jesus, and your Catholic church, says you are. You can either choose to embrace that identity or you can choose to reject that identity.

And then you can see where your priorities line up.

Growing up as a little Catholic kid in southern California, I never read the Bible. As a child, I never picked it up, I never read it. But, when I became a teenager, God placed a particular scripture in my mind and in my heart and He planted it so deep that I couldn't shake it.

I don't even know where I heard it. It must have been in one of the readings or one of the homilies at Sunday Mass, but it stuck with me. It's the gospel of Matthew, Chapter 6, Verse 24, where Jesus said, "No one can serve two masters."

Now that jumped out at me, and has always jumped out at me. Jesus didn't say some of us can serve two masters and some of us can't. Jesus said, "No one can serve two masters."

First of all, who are the masters that Jesus is talking about? Well, he's talking about himself, God, as the Master and all the values that Jesus holds up. The other master is the master of the world and all of the values of the world.

Now most of you have probably reached the point in your life, like I have in mine, that we begin to become very much aware that the values of Jesus and the values of the world are 180-degrees opposite.

That's why Jesus made it very clear that none of us can live our lives serving God and the world. We have to choose which master we're going to serve.

Having read that, I began to watch people to see which master they seemed to be serving. I watched my parents. I watched their friends. I just watched people in general. For the most part, this is often what I saw.

I saw people come into Mass for an hour on Sunday. If Mass lasted any longer than an hour they'd start looking at their watches. Some would become very agitated. Not everybody, but many of the people that I watched.

I could see they already had in their minds when they came to Mass that they were only going to serve God for one hour on Sunday.

And, those same people, who seemed to have a very difficult time worshiping and serving God for an hour on Sunday, would walk out of the doors of that church and spend 60, 70, 80 and even 90 hours a week serving that other master. So, as I grew up, I figured that must be what I'm supposed to do.

So, for much of my adult life, I would come into church for an hour on Sunday. Then, I would walk out of the doors of that church and I would spend 60, 70, 80, 90 and sometimes even 100 hours a week serving the master of the world and those values that the world holds up for each and every one of us each day.

As you know, billions of dollars are spent every year to get us to accept and to buy into those values. Narrowed down, all of the world's values that so many of us seek to serve fit into five major realms - money, power, possessions, recognition and authority.

The world tells you that if you have enough of those five things your life will be filled with peace, your life will be filled with hope and you will be "a success."

Remember the words of Blessed Mother Teresa of Calcutta. "We have not been placed on this earth to be successful; we have been placed on this earth to be faithful."

Actually, we're all going to be faithful to something. We're going to be faithful to Jesus or we're going to be faithful to the master of the world.

When I was growing up, however, it was the values of the world that sounded pretty good to me, not the values of Jesus. So I started pursuing the values of the world. And, I became a wonderful success - in the eyes of the world and in the minds of others who followed those same values.

However, I realized very quickly that it's impossible to walk toward two things at the same time.

As I began, with everything in me, to walk toward money and power, possessions, recognition and authority, I began to leave other things behind. I began to walk away from my relationship with God, my relationship with my church, my relationship with my bride, Linda, and my relationship with our two daughters, Christina and Kelly.

You see, I didn't have time for any of those things because I was out spending all of my time serving the master of the world. By the time I had reached 35 years old, I had achieved a level of success that I had never thought I'd ever achieve.

But, it was success as seen in the eyes of the world, certainly not in the eyes of God. I had ended up as vice president of the second largest military distribution company of its kind in the United States.

I had more money, more power, more possessions, more authority and more recognition than I ever thought I'd have.

To achieve that level, this had become my average work-week:

I'd get on an airplane on Sunday. I'd fly all over the country for meetings during the week. I'd return home on an airplane the following Friday. Then, I'd spend all day Saturday in my office doing paperwork. Sunday would roll around and I'd go to church.

For that hour on Sunday I would serve God. And then I would rush home and re-pack my suitcase. If I had any time left over, I'd spend what little time there was with Linda and the kids. Then, I was back on an airplane again. And, this routine went on for years and years and years.

Then, in one particular week in January of 1983, God gave me a spiritual wake-up call. I'm telling you, that spiritual wake-up call is what eventually led me to begin our missions and then to write this book.

Now, every one of us has had spiritual wake-up calls from God. We may not have realized what they were at the time but looking back we can easily recognize them. A spiritual wake-up call is very simply a time when our God creates a situation - or allows a situation to take place - to get our attention.

Listen for God's wake-up calls

A spiritual wake up call stops us right where we are.

And God makes it very clear that we are to look at our lives and see if what we are saying and what we are doing is giving Him glory.

You see, I believe, with everything in me, that the only reason we have been created is to give God glory by what we say and by what we do.

In that one particular week, I looked at my calendar and saw that it would be a little bit busier week than normal. I was going to be on nine airplanes, in eight cities, in six days.

Looking back on it, that was absolutely insane. But, I was so grounded, so rooted, in serving the master of the world that I looked at that schedule at that moment and it actually excited me.

So, on Sunday afternoon I flew from San Diego, Calif., to New York City.

The very next day I'm at a luncheon meeting with three other business men and myself in the Waldorf Astoria Hotel. That's a very famous, and very expensive hotel.

My luncheon bill for the four of us - and keep in mind this was in 1983 - my luncheon bill came to seven hundred and fifty-two dollars for the four of us!

Believe me, I'm not telling you this because I'm proud of it. I'm only trying to show you what kind of a life I was living in those years because of the master I had decided to serve. You need to know this to understand the spiritual message that God was about ready to give me.

So when the check came, I pulled out my American Express card - yes, I never left home without it - and I gave it to the waiter. You see I didn't care what the meal had cost because I wasn't paying for it. The company was paying for it.

After I said goodbye to the three other business men, I walked out of this world famous hotel, heading for the airport.

Now, some of you may have been to New York City or even lived there. New York is a very unusual city. One city block can be like rows of palaces and the next block may be like a slum.

As I walked out of this world famous Waldorf Astoria Hotel, I looked about halfway down the block and saw a cab. I started walking toward the cab, heading for the airport, and realized I had to keep stepping over sleeping homeless people to get to that cab. That made me very angry.

In fact, I remember literally screaming at them as I stepped over the homeless people lying on the street who were in my way.

"You worthless, lazy, shiftless no good bums," I shouted at them. "Get out of my way."

You see, at that time in my life, I saw no connection at all between me, and them, and God. They were just in my way. They were preventing me from getting to where I wanted to go as fast as I wanted to go.

That's when God burned this message into my heart.

God said, "Glenn, there's something wrong with this!"

But, still angry, I went on, got into the cab and arrived at the airport in time to catch my flight from New York City to San Francisco. After more meetings that day, I got up very early the next morning. I recall I had a 6:30 a.m. flight.

I'm in the airplane, on the runway, waiting to take off and I look out of the window of that airplane and folks, for the life of me, I could not remember what city I was in.

I was moving so fast that I could not remember where I was. I had to ask the passenger next to me. Well, that scared me. Once again God burned this message into my heart. He said, "Glenn, there's something wrong with this."

Well, that day I went to three other cities, first Denver, then Salt Lake City and I ended up in San Antonio, Texas, about 10:30 that night. I always stayed at the same hotel. So, I got a cab to the hotel and walked into the lobby. The desk clerk saw me, tossed my keys to me and up to the 40th floor I went.

I opened the door of my hotel suite, walked in and dropped my bag on the carpet. As the door closed behind me, I suddenly noticed the full-length mirror on the back of that door.

I stood there and I looked at myself.

Folks, I was 35 years old and I looked like I was 60.

And, I said - not in any kind of a formal prayer - "Lord, is this all there is?"

Have you ever said, "Oh, God, is this all there is?"

You see I had spent many, many years thinking that if I just had enough money and power, if I just had a high enough position on the corporate ladder, I would be filled with peace and joy.

Instead, my life was falling apart. And, I didn't know what to do.

So, I went to bed, I finished out my week and I was flying home on Friday. As I'm sitting in the airplane, flying back to San Diego, I was reflecting on that past week. I knew something had happened to me that week. I didn't know what it was. I didn't know who had caused it to happen. But there was something stirring within me that had never been there before.

Well, the plane landed in San Diego, I drove home, I pulled into my driveway and got out of my car. At this point, there's something you need to know about the relationship I had at that time in my life with my bride, Linda.

We'd been married for 13 years and we had two very beautiful daughters.

Way back then, Linda would go to all of the spiritual things. She went to Bible study, she went to prayer meetings and she'd just been to this mission at our church. As you might imagine, at that time in my life, you would have never caught me at a parish mission. And, Linda knew that.

So when I opened the front door it must have taken a tremendous amount of courage and faith for my bride to ask me this question.

"Glenn," she said, "there's a Catholic evangelist giving a parish mission in our church. Would you like to go?"

"I'll give the guy one night!"

Now, see, normally I would have cut her off halfway through her sentence and said absolutely not! But because something was stirring within me I looked at her and said very carefully, "How long is he going to be there?"

She said, "He's going to be there all week."

"I'll give the guy one night," I said.

Since Linda and I have been doing these missions, as Catholic evangelists, I've come to realize that almost everyone who comes to our missions is saying - and thinking - "I'm going to give this guy one night."

And, if you told any of your friends, they probably said, "Are you going? Tell me if he's any good. Maybe I'll come tomorrow night."

Well, needless to say, I stayed the entire week.

And, folks, I'm telling you I heard things at that mission that made my mind say, "Tilt! Do not listen to this!"

That's why Jesus told us to renew our minds. You see, Jesus knew that this mind of ours would be the source of a lot of our problems. If we did not renew it to get on the right track we would be in deep trouble.

Fortunately, that night, while my mind was saying "Tilt, do not listen to this!", my heart and my spirit were rejoicing. Because my heart and my spirit had been wanting to hear the messages of an evangelist like him for 35 years.

I just would not slow my life down long enough to listen. So God created the right situation and he stopped me.

At that mission, I heard many, many things that changed my life forever.

And you're going to read many things in this book that, if you will take it in, if you will renew your mind, and let it penetrate your heart and spirit, it will change your life forever.

There was one specific thing that I heard at that mission that changed my whole understanding of who I was. It set me on a new path, as a Catholic evangelist, and led me to become an ordained Deacon in our Catholic church. I want to share it with you. In a loving, caring way, I hope it turns your life upside down just like it did mine.

I'm going to assume that most of you who read this book have heard of the Second Vatican Council. It happened between 1962 and 1965, when 2,500 bishops from around the world gathered together in Rome and reviewed every aspect of the Catholic church.

These bishops wrote a lot of documents at that council, but I wonder how many of you are aware of the significance of one small little document they wrote. It's the document on the laity from Vatican II.

Very simply, and quite powerfully, the Holy Spirit used those bishops to tell the laity of the church their true identify and how they could live out that identify.

And I want to share one paragraph with you, because when I heard this I tell you it changed my life.

Now these words are not the words of Deacon Glenn Harmon. Those would be easy to reject. But these are the words of our own Catholic bishops. They say to you as laity that "from the fact of their union with Christ ... flows the lay person's right and duty to be apostles. It is by the Lord himself that they, the laity, have been called to this Apostolate."

I heard that and in my mind I said, "Stop the train." This was big news to me.

Later, I had the privilege, some 20 years ago, to visit with two or three of the bishops who had gone to that second Vatican council and, being a lay person at the time, I asked them:

"Are you telling me that because of my union with Jesus Christ through my baptism, the same Jesus who established this church, that Glenn Harmon as a Catholic layman has a right and duty to be an apostle, just like the early apostles?"

Those bishops grinned and said, "That's exactly what we're saying."

I said, "Will you help me understand this. You see, I've never heard that before.""Glenn," they said, "those early apostles that Jesus gathered together were created for a special moment in time to do a special work.

They're gone. And, they're not coming back. You see, they've already done what God asked them to do.

"Glenn, you are one of the modern day apostles. You have been created for this moment in time. And, as Jesus said, you are called to do even greater work."

One of the reasons I had such a difficult time wrapping my brain around that concept is that I had grown up in a church that was like a cathedral. As a little boy growing up I'd look up at the stained glass windows, at all of those holy women and men in the early church, and I'd say to myself, "Oh, Lord, I could never be like them."

But, think about it.

Who did Jesus choose to do His work, to be His apostles?

He chose ordinary people.

And, when those ordinary people surrendered everything to Jesus, when they made themselves available to Jesus Christ, He took those ordinary people and turned them into extraordinary people who did extraordinary things.

So, if you think that you are ordinary, well, praise God, because you are exactly who Jesus and our church is looking for today.

Don't be afraid of being an apostle. The word apostle simply means messenger, one who is sent. And each of us are going to be a messenger of something every day of our lives. We are going to project and preach and live some kind of a message. What kind of a message are you living today?

How have you lived with your husbands or wives, your children, your grandchildren, the people at work, the people in your church, your neighbors?

Have you lifted up the message of Jesus by what you have said and what you have done?

Or, have you been a messenger of the values of the world? Remember, we're all going to be messengers of something.

Now you know that our bishops tell us, because of our union with Jesus Christ, that all of the laity are apostles. After hearing this during one of our missions, many people will come up to me and say, "Glenn, if I accept and embrace my identity as an apostle, am I supposed to do what you do?"

27

Well, I don't know. Maybe God is raising you up at this moment in time to preach the good news of Jesus and the blessings of our Catholic church. What is more likely, I have found over the years, is that Jesus is calling you to be an apostle right where you are.

In your marriage, with your children, your grandchildren, for the people at work, the people in your neighborhood. Jesus is calling you to be that messenger, that apostle, who portrays the messages of the Gospel of Jesus Christ. Regardless of your role in life, I want you to realize that your true identity is as an apostle of our Lord, Jesus Christ.

You may be a doctor, you may be a teacher, you may be a lawyer, a plumber, a firefighter or a police officer but that is what you do. That is not who you are. Really, it makes no difference what you do in your life, you can be an apostle wherever you are and whatever your do.

So often we place our entire identity in what we do. Have you ever known somebody who after many, many years either retires, or they lose their job for one reason or another, and they just seem to fall apart.

They fall apart because all of their identity was in their job, in what they did for a living.

So, I want you to know, from this moment forward, that your true identity, because of your union with Jesus Christ, is that you are an apostle. Now, you have to look at your priorities in a new way. Look at this moment in your life and see if your priorities line up as being an apostle of Jesus Christ.

It's often not easy to do. You can't expect to make that change completely overnight.

After I heard at that mission with Linda about our Christian apostleship, it took me eight years to totally believe, completely accept and completely embrace my identity as an apostle.

It took me that long very simply because I realized that what was coming out of my mouth everyday were not the words of an apostle of Jesus Christ. And, because the way I was living my life, in many cases, did not line up with the way an apostle of Jesus Christ would live their life.

And, I knew that if I accepted my identify I was going to have to surrender and change so that Jesus could use me to give Him glory.

I pray that you will, at some point, embrace your true identity as an apostle.

Now, finally, we come to our sixth roadblock.

Just to recap, we've had regret, shame and guilt of the past, which was roadblock number one.

We've talked about fear of the future, which was number two.

Number three was choosing to believe what other people say about you rather than what our Lord says about you.

Number four was not understanding our true identity given to us by Jesus and our Catholic church, which leads to the fifth roadblock, misplaced priorities.

And, last, we come to roadblock number six - rejection!

I have to tell you, this has been the most difficult one for me to deal with and to overcome.

None of us want to be rejected, do we? Most of us want to be liked. In fact, many people spend their entire life trying to please others just to be liked by them.

They run around saying just tell me what you want me to say, tell me what you want me to do, tell me how you want me to dress, tell me how you want me live, just, please, like me.

Don't reject me.

And, so often, this roadblock of rejection has to do with fearing to share our faith.

I don't think that there is any Christian who would find it a major revelation that Jesus has called each and every one of us to go and share our faith.

But, so often we don't do it because we are concerned about being rejected by others. Because we don't want to be rejected, we don't want to share our faith.

As a result, millions of people die in this world every year without ever knowing Jesus Christ because the people who say they know and love Jesus Christ refuse to share that love of Jesus with others.

Here's an example from my own life.

I grew up with two very beautiful parents. My mom was a Catholic Christian woman and my dad was a wonderful man. He wasn't a Catholic, although he was a baptized Christian. I saw him in church only twice in my entire life. The first time was when Linda and I got married. The second time he was in a church was at his own funeral.

When I was growing up as a little Catholic kid in San Diego, Calif., my mom didn't know how to drive. So Dad would drive my mom and I to church every Sunday morning for Mass.

But, he'd wait out in the car.

I'll never forget this one particular Sunday morning. Mass was over. Dad, as usual, was sitting in the car out in the parking lot. We got in the car and Dad started driving home.

Now, remember, I was five years old. At this age, when you have a question, you just ask it. You don't care if it's the right question. You don't care if the time is right.

You think of a question and out it comes.

I remember my dad was sitting in the driver's seat, my mom was riding in the passenger seat and I was sitting in the back, when I said, very calmly, and very innocently, "Dad, why don't you go to church with Mom and me?"

Oh, I'm telling you, that was the wrong question to ask.

I saw my mom's shoulders tense up. I got very quiet. Dad didn't answer me in the car. In fact, my dad didn't answer that question until nearly two hours later, when he came to see me while I was playing in my room.

Dad came in, sat down and said, "Glenn, you know that question you asked me in the car, about why I don't go to church with your mother and you?"

I said, "Yes, sir."

He said, "I believe in God. Just don't ever talk to me about Him." Now, at five years old, you want to be obedient to your parents. You want to do what they say. So from that time on, I never did talk to my Dad about God.

In October of 1991, my Dad was 76 years old, and he was dying. He was dying from just about everything a person could die from. He had cancer throughout his entire body. He had smoked for over 40 years which left him with only 20 percent of his lungs remaining. And, because it was so hard for him to breath, his heart was beginning to weaken.

My mom had gone to be with the Lord 10 years before that, so when my dad reached the point where he could no longer take care of himself medically, Linda and I invited him to come live with us, which he accepted.

Let me tell you, it was a marvelous experience, especially for our two teenage daughters. For one thing, they saw up close and personal that nobody is immortal, not even their grandfather.

Well, after nine months my dad had reached the point where we couldn't give him the care he needed. So I had a real tough decision. I put him in a convalescent hospital. I'd visit him four or five times a week. He had his good days and he had his not so good days.

But, this one particular day I went to see my dad and he was having a miserable day. When I left his room, I started walking down the hall of that hospital and I began to have an intense conversation with God.

Ever have one of those intense conversations with God?

I was angry.

"God, why are you keeping my father here?" I asked Him. He's lonely. He's miserable. He's hurting every day."

Well, even today, I can take you to the exact spot in that hallway where God burned this message in my heart.

"Glenn, I'm keeping him here so you can tell him about my son, Jesus."

I remember thinking, "Oh, no!"

That's when I reminded God of what I could never forget.

I reminded him that when I was five years old, Dad told me, "Don't you ever, ever, ever talk to me about God!"

"Lord, what if he gets angry with me? Oh, Lord, what if he rejects me? What if he finally rejects you?" I asked.

Then, in frustration, I remember telling God that He's going to have to figure out a new way.

You see at that time in my life, I was so arrogant with God that I thought if I said, "Lord, you're going to have to figure out another way," then God would say, "Oh, Glenn, I'm so sorry to have bothered you. I'll work it out some other way."

But, for the next week, it didn't make any difference where I was, at home, in the car or at work, I must have heard God's same message 20 times a day.

"Tell your dad about my son, Jesus."

One day I had a morning like I know you've had at times in your life, where God has been urging, nudging and poking you to get you to do something that's important.

And, you just kind of pretend you're not hearing him.

That morning, when I woke up, I just knew I was going to have to do what God had been asking me to do.

Later that day, after work, I headed for the hospital. It was about a 20-minute drive. Well, 10 minutes into that drive my hands were so sweaty I could hardly hold onto that steering wheel.

You see, rather than seeing this as a glorious resurrection moment, I saw it as a crucifixion moment. And, I said the same thing that Jesus said in the garden of Gethsemane. I said, "Oh, Lord. Can we figure out another way?"

When I got to the hospital, I was still thinking, "Lord, I don't want to do this."

So I got to that hospital and I started walking down that long hallway. Now at that moment, in my mind, there were a couple of things that I was thinking about. I knew that I did a very poor job of living these two things, but I sure did know about them.

The first thing was that everything we are supposed to do on this Earth should be motivated by love - love of God and love of one another.

Well, if love is the motivator, then, my brothers and sisters, faith is the activator. Faith is what kicks it all into gear. Faith is what makes it happen. I remember getting to the door of my father's hospital room and under my breath I remember saying, "God, I don't think I have enough faith to do this."

Then, in those quiet places of our hearts where you hear God speak to you, God said, "Glenn, you make the effort and I will bless it."

Now, when I heard that, I had no idea what that meant.

Then, I opened the door of my Dad's hospital room and prepared to step in.

First, there is something you should know about my Dad at that particular moment in his life.

He was so lonely and so miserable that the first thing he did every morning about 5 am. would be to reach over, grab the remote control for the television set and turn it on. It would stay on all morning, all afternoon and into the late, late night. About 11:30 p.m. he would pick up that remote again and turn off the television.

So, it was no surprise to me that when I walked into his room the television was blaring away. I sat down in the chair beside his bed. Quite honestly I began to talk to Dad about everything except what I was there to talk about.

"Nice weather, huh, Dad? How about that football game today, Dad?"

God said, "Get with it!"

Has God ever said, "Get with it!" to you when you hesitated to do what you knew needed to be done? Well, I got up and I sat on my Dad's bed. I looked at him and said, "Dad, I'm here tonight to talk to you about something."

Miracle number one:

Dad reached over, grabbed the remote control of the television and turned it off.

Miracle number two:

Dad looked at me and said, "What do you want, Son?"

You see, in over 40 years, my Dad had never called me "Son."

I looked at him and said, "Dad, I'm nervous and I'm afraid, but I'm here tonight to share with you about Jesus Christ."

Then, this little 76-year-old man, who was literally skin and bones, began to cry. With tears running down his cheeks, he said, "Oh, thank God. I was hoping somebody would talk to me about Jesus."

"Dad, are you serious?" I said.

"Glenn, more than anything in my life," he said.

Knowing that my Dad didn't have much time left, I started talking to him about Jesus.

"Dad, I want you to repeat after me. Lord Jesus, I am sorry for my sins. I acknowledge you as the son of the living God and I accept you as my Lord and my God. I invite you into every area of my life this night and I receive you as my Lord and my Savior. Fill me with your Holy Spirit. Heal me. Strengthen me. I love you, Jesus."

When Dad got through repeating those words, he surprised me again.

"Glenn," he asked, "Would you write that down? I want to say it every day."

Three weeks later, Dad died.

Today, as you read this, I believe with everything in me that my dad is in heaven with my mom, and that he's looking down at me and saying, "Look God, there, that's my son, who risked all his fears of rejection to share you with me."

Right now, think about who in your life needs to hear about Jesus Christ.

Most of us don't even have to go outside of our household to find that person. Maybe it's a wife or a husband, a son or daughter or a brother or a sister. Maybe it's somebody at work or maybe it's your neighbor.

Do you love God enough, do you love that person enough, to risk any kind of rejection to share your faith in Jesus Christ with them?

Maybe, God would have worked out another way with my Dad. But, you see, I love God and I realized that I loved my Dad too much to take that chance.

As apostles, we are called to be messengers of Jesus Christ. In every day of our lives God brings at least one person into our path so we can share Jesus with them.

Now, if we don't realize our true identity as an apostle, and if we are so terribly afraid of rejection, we will never live out God's will in those situations. As a result, many people who may need Jesus Christ will never hear about Him, at least not from you.

Today, finally, I have become so accustomed to my identity as an apostle, I am constantly on the lookout for that person.

In my mind, I'm always aware and searching.

"Lord, is that the person? Lord, am I supposed to share you with that person?"

You see, I'm constantly looking for opportunities to make myself available to do the work of Jesus.

As we end these thoughts about life's true roadblocks to victory in our spiritual life, I know that every reader of this book - just like every person who attends one of our missions - is struggling with at least one of these roadblocks.

I ask you to pray, perhaps as you've never prayed before in your life, asking God to give you the faith and the courage you need to surrender whatever it is that you're holding on to that's keeping you from moving closer to God's embrace.

And, always remember the importance of the sacrament of the present moment. Living in the past or living in the future steals from the present.

Let's end this chapter
with a prayer...

Lord, give us new wisdom and insight to understand our true identity. We ask by the power of the Holy Spirit that the loving lessons in this book will leave us prepared to go out into our world as your apostles.

We ask all of these prayers, all of these petitions and offer all of these desires of our heart in the name of your Son, our Lord and Savior, Jesus Christ.

Amen

Your 5-Step Process
for Surrender

Throughout our lives, our Lord asks us to surrender certain things.
He doesn't do this for His benefit, but for ours.

He knows that if we will, we will truly find the peace and freedom we desire.

Over my life I have made the decision to surrender many things to my Lord: regret, guilt, shame, fear, anger, sin, bitterness, resentment, unforgiveness - and the list goes on and on.

Surrender is not easy.

Many people see surrender as a sign of weakness.

But when it involves God and us, surrender is a sign of strength and obedience.

For over 20 years, I have used this process to let go and surrender to God.

IT WORKS!

I'm sharing it with you in the hope that you will use it to gain the abundant life that our Lord wants for you.

1. Come to an acceptance and understanding that you have things to surrender. People who might consider themselves "perfectionists," or people who like to be "in control" often find this is a very difficult step.
2. Name the things you have to surrender; make a list.
3. Begin to imagine what your life would be like if you were not carrying those burdensome things around everyday. Think about the peace, joy, hope, love and freedom you would begin to experience.
4. At this point in your life, why are you not letting these things go?
5. This is the most difficult step for most people. Quite often a good spiritual director is needed to help you "peel the onion" to uncover those reasons.
6. Then, let those things go and surrender them to God.

A Call To Action

We believe that faith is acting on what we say we believe. We invite you to "review" and "act" on the reflection questions listed below. We wish you God's blessings!

1. How did you answer the three questions at the beginning of this chapter? What do your answers say to you about your understanding and relationship with Jesus Christ?
2. Which one of the six roadblocks discussed in this chapter is causing the most difficulty in your life right now?
3. What action can you take to remove it from your life?
4. What was your reaction when you realized that because of your "union" with Jesus Christ, your true identity is as an apostle?
5. What priorities can you re-arrange to better live out your identity as an apostle?
6. What is the number one thing that God is asking you to surrender?
7. How can you use the 5-step process for surrender to accomplish your goal?

Chapter 2

Our True Purpose, God's Will For Our Lives

God always knows exactly what you need in your life.

So you can be sure He is planting seeds of faith in your heart and mind as you read these words.

That's why I want to talk to you about God's will for our lives, mine and yours, because He sees, far more clearly than we do, what He wants for each one of His children and the paths He wants us to follow.

Now, I'm sure each one of you is a prayerful person who each and every day prays to our Lord and asks God to do something for you, or for someone that you love and care about.

You may have been praying that same prayer for months or even years. And, even though you've been very faithful to whatever that prayer is, at this present moment you see no evidence that God is going to answer your prayer.

And when we reach that point, where we pray and pray and pray and nothing we can see or hear or touch is telling us that God is going to answer that prayer, we get real honest with ourselves and we begin to doubt.

If you recall, one of the greatest saints, St. Thomas, doubted. It's natural. It's a human thing to do.

So, at different times in our lives, when we begin to doubt that we're not praying right, or that our prayers are not reaching where they're supposed to go, that's when it's extremely important that we stand on the promises of God.

Just to reinforce that thought, turn in your Bible to the book of Sirach, in the Old Testament, and turn to Chapter 35, beginning with verse 16.

Now, I can remember many years ago I had been praying and praying for something and one day I began to doubt. I doubted not only that my prayers were even reaching where it was supposed to go, but I also doubted that God was ever going to answer my prayers.

That's when I ran across this promise from God. And, my brothers and sisters, I stood on this promise until God finally answered my prayers.

For you, too, this Bible passage is a promise from God that you can depend on.

Verse 16 begins...

"He who serves God willingly is heard. His petition reaches the heavens. The prayer of the lowly pierces the clouds. It does not rest until it reaches its goal. Nor, will it withdraw until the Most High responds."

That promise from God is telling each and every one of us that, if we are serving God willingly, our Lord hears us when we pray. Our prayers reach where we want them to go, right into the throne room of Almighty God. And, they stay there, until God responds to our prayers.

What a powerful promise from God!

So whatever you're praying for, in your life or in the life of someone you love and care about, God promises that as long as you are serving him willingly, He will hear you and will - at the right time - answer your prayers.

When we pray to God, we are praying to that same God who made those promises to Sirach.

That gives us assurance that as individual people, in a community of faith, we can lay our petitions, our desires, our hopes, our dreams, our fears and our doubts at God's feet.

We should always ask God to grant all of our prayers, according to His will, and that we will have the patience to wait for His answer.

We should also ask God to give us the faith to accept whatever His answer is, and the courage to continue to live our lives according to the gospel of our Lord, Jesus Christ.

Now, when I talk about God's true purpose, His will for our lives, I'm not talking about what kind of clothes you should be wearing.

I'm not talking about what kind of a car you should drive or what size of a house you should live in, or what kind of a job you should have.

When I talk about God's will for our lives I'm referring to the root reasons why we have been created by Almighty God to be on this earth.

Why is doing God's will so hard?

This whole thing about doing God's will has been a problem for human beings since the beginning of time. You can go all the way back to the Garden of Eden, when God created Adam and Eve.

God looked at Adam and Eve and told them, "Everything you can see, as far as the eye can see, is yours. I give it to you, enjoy it and be blessed by it."

But, God said, "There's that one little tree over there that you can't touch."

You see, that was God's will for Adam and Eve.

Of course, we all know that Adam and Eve decided they knew better than God, that their will was superior to God's will.

As you know, we've all been paying the price for their decision ever since.

So, please keep an open mind and an open heart as I share what I believe God's will is for each of our lives.

You see, for the first 35 years of my life, I lived as though God had said, "Glenn's will be done." I was doing just fine. I was a self-made man.

As I told you earlier, I worked 70, 80, 90, even 100 hours a week for what I wanted, but I said, "God, I'll give you one hour a week. I'll come to church, I'll pray, I'll stand, I'll kneel. I'll sing, I'll say all the prayers but when I walk out of the doors of this church you don't bother me and I won't bother you...unless I want something, and then, God, I'll ask you for it and I'll expect you'll give it to me. And, once you do, we'll go back to 'I won't bother you and you don't bother me,' all right?"

You see, I believed that I didn't need God in my life. Maybe that's where you're at in your life, too.

I had reached the point in my life where I had everything the world told me I needed to be happy. But, believe me, I wasn't happy.

One day, in desperation, I cried out to God, "Lord, what is your will for my life?"

Well, I discovered that God had been waiting 35 years for me to ask that question.

You see, we were created by a very patient God. He doesn't push, he doesn't shove, he doesn't manipulate. He just waits, with His arms outstretched, waiting for us to finally reach the point where we are ready to come to Him.

Well, as soon as those words came out of my mouth, as soon as I said, "Lord, what is your will for my life?" I was humbled beyond belief.

I was a 35-year old Catholic Christian man and not only didn't I know what God's will was for my life, but I had no idea where to go to find it.

That humbled me.

But, it also began a very personal journey that eventually led me to devote my life to bringing God's messages to people in churches all over the United States and Canada - and inspired me to write this book to share God's message with you.

When I realized that I had no idea about where to find the answer to my question, the first place I went was to the last place I ever thought I would actually go to discover God's will for my life - a dictionary.

You see, God can use anything to reach us if we will just crack that door open a little bit to let Him in.

When I picked up Webster's Dictionary, I found what the dictionary said about the word "will," which it defined as "the power of making a reasoned choice or controlling one's own actions."

Now, when I read that definition I picked up two words I focused on, "choice" and "actions."

I figured if I ever did stumble onto God's will for my life I was going to have to make a choice. I was either going to have to choose to do it or I was going to have to choose to reject it. And, whatever my choice was, I was going to have to act on it.

Do you realize that every day of our lives, we make a choice to either do God's will or we make a choice to reject it?

Whatever our choice is, we will then act on that choice.

I still didn't know what God's will was for my life, but I felt that I had made a major step toward understanding what I would have to do when I discovered His will. Then, I did something that I had never done before in my life.

I went into a bookstore to find a spiritual book.

During all of the many years when I was immersed in the world of high-level business, seeking what society told me should be my goals, I had all kinds of time to read things like the Wall Street Journal, Fortune 500 magazine and Golf Digest, but I could never quite find the time to read a spiritual book.

While browsing the store's bookshelves, I came across a book called "The Road Less Traveled," by M. Scott Peck. Some reviewers have said that perhaps no book in this generation has had a more profound impact on our intellectual and spiritual lives. It has sold more than seven million copies in the United States and Canada, it's been translated into more than 23 languages and stayed on the New York Times "bestseller" list for more than 20 years.

In that book, the author offered his own definition of the word "will." He said that "will" is a desire of sufficient intensity that that intensity is translated into action.

There's that word "action" again, along with two new words, "choice" and "intensity."

When I discovered God's will for my life, I knew I would have to choose to do it, and I was going to have to do it with everything in me, with all the intensity I could muster.

Well, I spent about six months turning over every rock to try to discover God's will for my life. During that time, a good friend of mine, a good Christian friend, had been watching me go through this journey. And one day he walked up to me and said, "Glenn, have you ever read this book?"

The book he was holding up was the Bible.

Well, I was very honest with him. I said, "No, I have never read that book."

He handed it to me and said, "I think if you take this home and begin to study it and reflect on it, I think it will help you discover God's will for your life."

So, I took that Bible, the holy living word of God, home with me and that evening I sat down on the sofa to read it.

Once again, I was humbled.

I didn't know what to do with that Bible.

It's the most important book ever written but I didn't know what to do with it.

I didn't know whether to read it like a novel, you know, start with Genesis and go all the way through to Revelations, or pick a chapter in the middle that looked interesting and start there.

So, as I sat on the sofa, I said, "Oh, Lord, please help me. You know the desire of my heart. I want to serve you and you know I'm searching to find what you want for my life."

Thinking back about that moment, I realize that could very well have been the most honest prayer I had ever prayed in my life.

Before I move on, it's important that I mention how important the Bible is in our lives and how to approach it, if, like me, you're inspired to read the Bible for the first time.

Generally, when I ask people who the Bible was written for, they will say things such as "us," or "the body of Christ, the church."

Those are good answers but I don't believe either of those is the best answer. I believe the best answer is that the Bible is written for you!

You see, when you're thinking of the word "you" as you begin to read, the Bible becomes very personal to you.

For the first 35 years of my life, I did not believe that the Bible was written for me. But when I became convinced that it was written for me, then it meant that every book, every chapter, every verse and every word is written for "me."

Of course, that also means it was written for "you," for each member of your family, for each person who picks up the Bible and willingly follows Jesus.

The next time you're in church, when either the Priest or the Deacon or the Lector stands at the pulpit and is about to read the Word of God, I would invite you - in your mind - to tell yourself that what you are about to hear is written for "you."

My brothers and sisters, that thought will change your entire understanding, your entire focus on the Word of God that's contained in His Bible.

I don't want you to think that it's addressed to the person behind you, or in front of you or to either side of you. I want you to say, to yourself, "What I am about to hear is written for me." Because that's exactly why God inspired his apostles to write about his life here on Earth with us, and why he inspired his other children who wrote the Old Testament.

The Bible is simply full of messages from God to His people that He wants you to read, things He wants you to know, encouragement He wants to offer you at difficult times and His thoughts that make the Bible a guide book for living your life.

When I sat on that sofa, many years ago, saying, "Lord, please help me," God led me to the Gospel of John, in the New Testament, the fifth chapter, verse 38. Please turn to that scripture and you'll see what Jesus said to me.

"For I have come down from heaven, not to do my own will but to do the will of Him who sent me."

You see, at that point in my life I had a very poor relationship with Jesus. I knew about Jesus, but I didn't really know Jesus.

I also knew that Jesus and I have the same Father - God, the Father of us all.

Well, if Jesus was the messenger of the will of His Father then what Jesus said must be what I am supposed to do. I believe that's why Jesus prayed so much. He didn't do anything until He prayed and asked His Father if that's what He wanted Him to do.

Father, do you want me to say this? Father, do you want me to go to this town? Father, do you want me to heal this man? Jesus didn't do anything until He knew it was the will of His Father in heaven.

That was a powerful scripture for me.

I still didn't know what God's will was for my life but I was making major strides toward discovering the truths that would change my life, change the way I lived.

Through all of this period, my prayer life was growing. My understanding of scripture was growing. My understanding of my Catholic faith was growing.

But, through all of this, in those really quiet places in my heart where God really speaks to each of us, I kept hearing God saying over and over and over again:

"Glenn, you're looking in the wrong place."

Now, I had no idea what God was trying to tell me in my search. What I didn't realize then, but I realize now, was where God was telling me to look.

So, I'm asking you, dear reader, to look in the same place. God was telling me to look in my heart. And, oh, it was dark in my heart.

There were areas of my heart that I had locked up, that I had closed and bolted, places where I had put "No Trespassing" signs in those darkest areas of my heart. I stayed out of those areas, I made sure no one else probed any of those areas and if I could have kept God out of those "off limits" places in my heart I would have kept Him out of it, too.

But, God told me, "If you want to find my will for your life you need to look into your heart."

So, that's why I ask you, what areas of your heart have you locked, bolted and shut tight and refused to go into, areas you don't even want God to see?

Of course, the only reason I had locked those areas of my heart is that some things had happened in the past that were very painful. I don't know about you, but I'm not crazy about pain. I will take all of the resurrection moments that I can get, but I will stay as far away as I can from those crucifixion moments.

I thought, of course, that if I just locked away those troubled areas of my heart they'd go way. But, they didn't. So, perhaps like you, I struggled with those memories and experiences for a long time.

And, during those struggles, as I was beginning to go on this journey to discover God's will for my life - the same journey we all go on at sometime during our lives, whether you realize that now or not - one of the things I did was to become a Hospice care volunteer.

I don't know if you know what Hospice is about. If you aren't familiar with it, Hospice is an international organization that ministers to people who are terminally ill. In most parts of the world, people who have been diagnosed by their doctor to have a year or less to live are eligible to be in Hospice care.

In my work with Hospice, I found it amazing what people begin to see as priorities when they know they don't have long to live in this world.

When I'd go to visit people who knew their time to die was close, some of them had only a week or 10 days left, I never heard one person say, "Glenn, I wish I'd had a bigger house, I wish I'd had a faster car or more money in the bank or a higher position in my corporation."

I never heard that.

But, what I did hear was, "I wish I had a better relationship with God," "I wish I'd spent more time serving my church or spent more time with my husband or wife, my children or my grandchildren."

So often, God's children wait until they are almost out of here before they truly realize what's important while they're on this earth?

I'll never forget this one man I met, Marvin. A Hospice director invited me to go see him. I remember Marvin for many reasons. First of all, because his name was Marvin. That was my Dad's name.

Before I went out to meet Marvin, she told me he only had perhaps 24 hours left to live. His time was really close. I drove out to Marvin's house, knocked on the front door and his wife came to greet me and invited me in. There must have been 30 family members gathered in the front room. His entire family had gathered together because they knew his time was short.

It took me hours to get past the family members to see Marvin. You see the family was dying, too, so I stayed to talk to them in their time of sorrow. Often, people are so intent to see and help the patient that they go right past the family, close friends and other caregivers. They need help and comforting, too, and talking to someone outside of the family often helps them express their thoughts and feelings.

When I finally got past everyone to see Marvin, he was really doing surprisingly well. So I started visiting with him. No matter how long our conversations were, I always got around to asking dying patients two questions that I believe are very important for a person to talk about at that moment in their lives.

They are also healing questions.

"Marvin," I said, "May I ask you, would you share with me some of the joys of your life?"

Oh, when I said that his face just lit up.

It glowed with happiness.

He must have spent the next 30 minutes telling me about all of the joys of his life - his family, the vacations they went on, all the wonderful memories he carried with him in his mind and heart. He just went on and on and on, enjoying recalling them and sharing them with me.

When he was through sharing all of those joys, I said, "Marvin, may I ask you, do you have any regrets?"

For a minute, he sat and thought about what I'd asked him.

Then he said, "Glenn, I have one."

"Marvin, may I ask you what it is?"

As he hesitated, I noticed a little tear roll down his cheek.

"Glenn, the only regret I have in my life is that I wish I would have loved more," Marvin said, sadly.

When he said that, as I was standing near his bed, something happened to me that I can never explain. Suddenly, my knees almost buckled out from under me. There was a chair nearby and I sat down and spent a few more minutes visiting with Marvin before I left. I knew I would never see Marvin again.

I spent a little more time with the family and then I left and started walking toward my car.

Now, I want you to realize that it had been more than a year at that point since I had begun my journey to discover God's will for my life. I had been turning over every rock , going down every road I could find.

Reaching my car, I took the keys out of my pocket, put them in the door, opened it and got in behind the steering wheel. Just as I was about ready to put the keys in the ignition, I heard God speaking to me. Now, I want to emphasize this to you. I have never heard the voice of God out loud, like I would hear you or another human being.

When I say I have heard God I am speaking about sensing Him speaking to me in the quiet places of my heart, where God really speaks to you. If that has happened to you, you know exactly what I mean. You see God speaks to each of us everyday in those quiet places of our heart.

But, so often, we're running around so fast, there is so much noise and clutter and we are so busy and preoccupied with life and living that we are never quiet.

That's why God said, in His Bible, "Be still and know that I am God."

God speaks to Glenn's heart

So, as I put my key into the ignition, I heard God say, "Glenn, that's it!"

Then, I said, "Lord, what's it?"

He said, "That's my will for your life, to love."

I said, "Oh God, that couldn't be it. That's too easy."

And God said, "Oh, really?!"

"Oh, Lord," I said, "I love my wife, Linda."

And God said, "Oh, do you?!"

"And, I love my two daughters, Christina and Kelly," I told Him.

I'll never forget what God said to me next.

"No. You don't!"

Well, I started up the car and I remember continuing to talk to God as I began to drive.

"No, Lord, I must not have heard you right," I told Him. And, I kept driving and thinking about what I'd heard God say to me.

Well, you know there are some people that God can just kind of walk up to and say, "Hello" and they hear him. I've discovered that sometimes God could walk up to me and hit me over the head with a two-by-four and I still just wouldn't get it.

Now, here's an important point I want you to really think about.

I realized that the main reason I didn't believe what God had just told me, the reason why I thought that His answer was far too easy, is that I thought I was going to have to go to some 700-page theological book on Catholic doctrine to find where I was going to discover God's will for my life.

Truthfully, the message of Jesus has always been, is today and will always be simple to understand.

He made His truth so simple that little kids could understand it.

But, there's a difference between the simplicity of understanding and the simplicity of doing.

So I kept going, trying to discover God's will for my life. Well, a few days later, during my usual scripture time, I ran across this scripture and I invite you to turn to it.

It's in the same Gospel of John, Chapter 13, Verses 34 and 35. And, this is what Jesus said to me, and what He also says to you.

"A new command I give you!"

I stopped right there. The first of the two words that jumped out at me was "new."

This was something that never had been said to me before.

Jesus was saying, "Folks, this is new, get ready."

The other word was command.

Jesus did not say He had a new "suggestion" to give you and me. Jesus did not say, "Now, you go home and talk about it and see if you want to do it."

Our Lord Jesus said "command."

When God says "command," He is serious.

And this is what He said next.

"Love one another as I have loved you. By this, all people will know that you are my disciples."

Once again, I was humbled beyond belief. I was a 35-year-old Catholic Christian man and I had no clue how God loved me.

Now, I'd heard, of course, all my life that God loves. God loves you. God loves me.

But, I had no idea how much. Jesus said I am to love each and every person as much as He loves me. Now, how could I possibly love you that way when I have no idea how God loves me?

Here's a suggestion for you to think about.

Starting tomorrow morning when you wake up, and for the next two weeks, think about this as you go through each day, everywhere you go and whatever you do.

If somebody was to just walk around with you every day, from the time you wake up in the morning until you go to bed at night, at the end of that two weeks would that person know that you are a disciple of

Jesus Christ simply, and only, by the way you love and by the way you allow others to love you?

Don't measure your conduct by even a single word that you say during those two weeks. That's not what's important.

You see, Jesus said others will know we are His disciples by the way we love and by the way we love others.

So, when I read that, I cried out to God, "Please tell me how you love me!"

And He led me to the book of Ephesians, Chapter 3, Verses 17-19. This is what God said to me through His Holy Word, through His Bible.

"So that Christ may dwell in your heart through faith, I pray that you, being worthy and established in love, may have power together with all the saints to grasp how wide, how long, how high and how deep is the love of Christ."

And, I said, "Oh Lord, how high is your love for me?" He said, "Glenn, when you're celebrating, when you're having a great time, I'm there celebrating with you."

I said, "Lord, how wide is your love for me?"

"It covers every experience in your life," He said."

I said, "Lord, how long is your love for me?"

He said, "Glenn, it starts at the moment of your conception and it goes throughout all of eternity."

And, finally, I said, "Oh Lord, how deep is your love for me?"

"Glenn, when you're in one of those crucifixion moments, when you think you can't go on one more minute, when you just kind of want to pull the covers over your head and don't even want to get out of bed in the morning," He said, "that's when I'm holding you, that's when I'm loving you and embracing you the most."

My brothers and sisters who are reading this book, I want you to realize that it was at that moment that, for the first time in my life, I realized how much our God, our Creator, loves me -- and each one of you.

I also realized that's how much I'm supposed to love you.

But I wasn't prepared, at that moment in my life, to choose what God had told me was His will for my life. So, I asked Him another important question about love.

"Lord, if love is your will for my life, how important is love?"

Take another look at First Corinthians, Chapter 13, Verses 1 through 3. This is what God said about the importance of love.

"If you speak in human and angelic tongues, but do not have love, you are a resounding gong or a clanging cymbal. If you have the gift of prophecy, and comprehend all mysteries and all knowledge, and have enough faith to move mountains, but you do not have love, you are nothing.

"If you give away everything you own and hand over your body so that you may boast, but you do not have love, you gain nothing."

That's what God told me when I read that scripture. I can have everything else the world says I need to have - and I had it folks - but if I don't have love I have nothing, I have gained nothing and I am nothing.

That tells me how important love is, in God's view.

During that heartfelt search to learn about God's love, I discovered something that I thought is really interesting about myself.

What's even more interesting, to me, is that as I've traveled this continent for many years conducting missions, I've discovered that we all do this to varying degrees. The best way I can explain this is to give you an example.

I'm sure that most of you, at one time or another in your life, have flown on an airplane. If for some reason you haven't, try to imagine this.

You're sitting on an airplane at the airport on a cloudy, rainy, ugly day. It's often depressing to many people. But as soon as your plane takes off and gains some altitude, it breaks through those clouds and once you get above them, it's sunny, it's bright and you even seem to feel better.

What just took place? What made the difference?

A cloud filtered out the beauty of the sun.

Each and everyone of us has put something around us that's invisible, something I call a "love filter."

We have put this love filter around us because we have been hurt by people - people we have trusted, people we have made ourselves vulnerable to, or we have been taken advantage of, or abused, we want to make sure that isn't going to happen again, because its painful.

So we put this love filter around us and we say to one another, "That's about as close as I'm going to let you get, because if I let you get any closer you might hurt me. I remember what that felt like and I am not going to allow that to happen.

Well, you see, we also do the same thing to God.

God's getting a little too close, we get a little nervous or uncomfortable and we back away.

I have become a firm believer that if we do not allow God to get love to us, God cannot get love through us. In other words, each one of us is a channel of His love, unless we block it with that love filter.

That's harmful to both us and anyone we come into contact with in our lives.

And to the degree that we allow God to love us is the exact degree that we are going to love one another.

In other words, on a scale of 1 to 10, with 10 being the greatest, if my life is going great, I wake up in the morning and say, "Oh, Lord, everything is wonderful; you can go ahead and love me with an '8' or a '9' today."

Folks, if that happens, I'm just going to love all over you.

But, if I wake up and my life is just going lousy, I'm miserable and I sense God getting a little too close and I say, "God, that's as close as I want you to get today, just love me with a '1' or a '2' today."

My brothers and sisters, in those times, just don't expect anything out of me.

You see Jesus is calling us to trust him enough, to trust one another enough to begin to dismantle that love filter. Because as long as that love filter is around us it is gong to block out the beauty and the graces and the blessings of God, the love of God and the love of one another.

So, I urge you to begin to believe and to trust in our Lord, Jesus. Begin to dismantle that love filter you think is protecting you. You see, we can get really confused, if we're not careful, with words.

Think about this.

If I was to say to you the word "wine," and I repeated it over and over and over again, "wine, wine, wine," at the end of 20 minutes of saying that word would I be intoxicated? Well, of course not!

So, if I can not become intoxicated by saying the word "wine," then can we love simply and only by saying the word "love?"

Absolutely not!

Now, I'm not saying we're not supposed to tell one another we love them. The human heart, the human spirit needs to hear each other say, "I love you."

But, how many times have you thought of saying to somebody, or you actually said to somebody, "Would you please stop telling me you love me because your actions don't match your words."

I think I can safely say that each and every one of you reading this can relate to what I just said.

You see, the problem with the word love in the English language is that we use the word "love" to describe all the different kinds of love. For example, I love my wife, I love my daughters, I love football, I love Cajun food.

For all kinds of love we use the same word, which means we can get real confused with the word "love" and what it really means.

I'm not sure if you are aware of this but in the Greek language there are many words used to describe love. And, I'll bet that you're not aware that you are very familiar with two of those words.

You didn't know that I knew you spoke Greek, did you? But the first of those two words is a four-letter word for love, called Eros. That is a reciprocal kind of love.

And, my brothers and sisters, that is the way most of us have been raised to understand "love" since we've been little children.

It is also the way the world teaches us to love.

If you will love me, I will love you.

If you stop loving me, I will stop loving you.

And, to the exact degree that you will love me, that's the degree to which I will love you back.

All of that is conditional love.

Remember when I told you that I told God I loved my wife, and He said, "Oh, do you?"

You see, Linda knew the boundaries she needed to stay in.

If she went outside of those boundaries, she could sense my love diminish. So long as she acted a certain way or talked a certain way or did things a certain way, everything was fine.

It was the same with my two daughters. I said I love my daughters, and God said to me, "No, you don't."

That's when I realized that I was putting so many conditions on my love for my daughters that they didn't know what to do. Just walking through the family room they probably broke one of the conditions of my love.

Conditional love can destroy a society. Please, let's take the conditions off of our love.

Just love one another

Now, the other Greek word we've all heard, a word that I've heard all my life and perhaps you have, too, is a word that I never fully realized what it meant until recently.

That is agape love, unconditional love.

Do you want an example of what that means?

Well, when I'm presenting these spiritual insights at our missions in Catholic churches across the United States and Canada there is always a Catholic crucifix hanging over the altar behind me.

If you will look at that Crucifix in your own church, in your home or anywhere a Crucifix is found, you will clearly see Jesus hanging on that cross.

That is unconditional love, agape love.

Jesus set no boundaries, no parameters, no limitations to His love. It's just flat out unconditional love.

What is so amazing to me is that more than 2,000 years ago Jesus went to the cross for me.

Yes, I said "for me" because I believe that He did that for me, and I can only speak for myself and what I believe.

As for you, and every person around the globe, you have to make your own decision. It's up to you to decide if you believe that Jesus went to the cross and died - for you. That is your personal decision, a conversation between you and God.

Once I believed that Jesus, 2000 years ago, died for me when He went to that cross, I realized that even then He knew exactly how I was going to treat Him for most of my life.

He knew there were going to be many times when I wanted nothing to do with Him. There were going to be many times that I was going to use His name in vain, many times when I wasn't even going to pray, when I didn't even care if He existed.

But, knowing that, He still went to the cross for me. He still suffered for me. He didn't say to me, Glenn, if you will act this way, if you will say these things, if you will do this or that or not do this or that, then I will go to the cross for you.

Jesus went to the cross for me in spite of all the things I did. And, in spite of all the things I continue to do.

That, my brothers and sisters, is unconditional love - agape love.

That's exactly why I'm writing this chapter, to tell you that "love" is God's will for each and very one of us.

Now, knowing this, you need to make a choice.

You're either going to do it or not do it. But, what ever your choice is, you're going to have to act on it. Personally, having ignored Jesus Christ and his love so much of my life, I chose to do what Christ asked.

So, then, I had to ask, "Oh, Lord, how am I supposed to love?"

Well, He showed me.

And, it hasn't all been easy.

I have to tell you that, quite honestly, there are times, even today, that I've wished that I had not asked Jesus that question. Because at times it was, and still is, very challenging to love as Jesus wants me to love.

In the first book of John, Chapter 4, Verse 8, it says that "God is love."

You see, love is an action and a decision for us.

But, for God, it is His character and nature. God only knows one way to love and that is unconditionally.

Now, remember the commandment that Jesus gave all of us in John 13.34.

"Love one another as I have loved you."

It is a two-part commandment. We cannot love others unless we know and understand how God loves us. To learn how God loves us, turn to the first book of Corinthians, Chapter 13, beginning with Verse 4.

"Love is patient."

I could see I was already in trouble. You see, I'm one of those people who says, "God, I want patience and I want it right now!"

Love is kind.

Love is not jealous.

Love is not pompous.

Love does not envy.

Love does not boast.

Love is not proud.

Love does not dishonor others.

Love is not self-seeking.

Love is not easily angered.

Love keeps no record of wrongs.

Love does not delight in evil but rejoices in the truth.

Love always protects, always hopes, always perseveres.

Love is not rude, love does not seek its own interest, love is not quick tempered, love does not brood over injury, love does not rejoice in wrong doing but rejoices in the truth.

Love bears all things, love believes all things, love hopes all things and love endures all things.

Since God is love, wherever the word "love" is, I will replace it with God. If you have ever wondered how God has and always will love you, after reading this you will never have to wonder or guess again.

God is patient.

When I look back over the six-plus decades of my life, I realize how patient God has been with me.

The first prayer I pray every morning is, "Lord, may everything I think, say and do today please you and give you the glory and honor you deserve." When I pray those words, I mean them with everything in me. But, not a day goes by that in some way or another I still just mess it up.

But, my Lord knows the desire of my heart and He gives me another day to get it right.

What a patient God we serve!

God is kind.

God is not jealous.

God is not pompous.

God is not inflated.

God is not rude.

God does not seek His own interests.

God is not quick tempered.

God does not brood over injuries.

God does not rejoice over wrong doing, but rejoices with the truth.

God bears all things.

God believes all things.

God hopes all things.

God endures all things.

Isn't that amazing!

God loves us in that way every second of every day of our lives.

WHAT AN AWESOME GOD!

But, even after I read all of this in God's Holy Bible, Jesus wasn't done with me yet.

He said, "Glenn, if you really want to do my will, if you truly want to be an apostle of mine, then wherever the word "love" is, put the word "I."

You see, Jesus wants us to make this very personal.

Try reading this out loud. As it penetrates your own mind and heart, you will discover where you are in your life with loving as Jesus wants us to love.

I am patient.

When I read this for the first time, I knew I was already in trouble. You see, I'm one of those people who says, "God, I want patience, and I want it right now!"

I am kind.

I am not jealous.

I am not pompous

I am not inflated.

I am not rude.

I do not seek my own interests.

I am not quick tempered.

And this next one was a big one for me to handle:

I do not brood over injuries.

I used to have 12 file cabinets in my heart where I had filed away all the things that people had done to hurt me over my life. Sure, I'd look at them and say, "I have forgiven you." But, at the same I'm thinking to myself, "Do you remember when you did this to me in 1985?"

Folks, if I was tempted to remind them of their actions, then I was not really forgiving them. I was still brooding over things that people had done to me many years before.

Remember, Jesus said, "Love does not brood over injury."

I continued down the list.

I do not rejoice over wrong doing but rejoice in the truth.

I bear all things.

I believe all things.

I hope all things.

I endure all things.

Well, when I thought about that last one, I got a little sick inside because I realized that at that moment in my life I was not living God's will for my life very well.

You see, I was learning that I had to make new choices in my life. I had to want, with everything in me, to go out there and love those people who are not easy to love.

As Christ has told us, it's easy to love somebody that you like, somebody who will love you back in the same way that you love them.

But, what about loving somebody patiently, without brooding over injury when they're not loving you the same way in return. I have come to believe that this whole message of love is exactly what was instrumental in getting Jesus to the cross.

Do you recall that point in scripture where Pontius Pilate was standing in front of the screaming crowd, with Barrabbas on one side of him and Jesus on the other, and he looked out over the crowd and said, "You can choose one of these men and whoever you choose I will let him go."

Now Barabbas was a revolutionary, and the crowd knew that. You see the Romans were raping their wives, they were beating their children, they were killing them, they were taxing them beyond belief and Barabbas cried out, "If you will let me go, we will do to those Romans exactly what they have done to us!"

You see, that's an eye-for-an-eye mentality. That's Eros love.

But Jesus looked at that same crowd and said these words that can be found in Luke's Gospel, Chapter 6, Verse 27. Now I want you to know, and remember, that these are not Deacon Glenn Harmon's words. These are the words of Jesus Christ.

He looked at that crowd and said, "Love your enemies, do good to those who hate you, bless those who curse you and pray for those who mistreat you."

This is agape love.

And those same people, that same crowd that had welcomed Jesus just a week earlier, on Palm Sunday, as their Savior, their Messiah, said, "This time, Jesus, you've gone too far."

And, they chose to set Barabbas free and send Jesus Christ to the cross.

Sadly, my brothers and sisters, absolutely nothing has changed in 2000 years.

When I make a conscious decision not to love somebody the way Jesus is calling me to love, once again I am - in essence - choosing Barabbas and sending Jesus right back to the cross.

As you read this book, think about this.

Who is your enemy?

Who is the hardest person for you to love?

Who is the hardest person for you to forgive?

You see, I can think of at least three or four people in my life who would cause me to say, "Oh, Lord, I will walk on hot coals for you but please do not ask me to love those people."

And, every time I think of them in that way, Jesus will come back and say, "Glenn, I love them and I have forgiven them. If you truly want to be a disciple and an apostle of mine you will have to love them and forgive them, too."

Before I move on, let me make a very important point about Eros love and agape love.

There is a difference between boundaries on love and boundaries on behavior.

Jesus Christ made it very clear in His Gospels how we are to live our lives. In other words, He has given us boundaries and has made it very clear what the consequences are for living outside of those boundaries.

But, no matter how we live, He will never stop loving us.

We can also have realistic and loving boundaries on behavior from those people in our lives - our spouse, children, grandchildren, relatives, co-workers, parents, etc. And, there can be consequences if they don't accept and live according to those boundaries.

But, whether they accept and live with those boundaries or not, we are still called to love them with an agape love.

Remember what I said. The Gospel teachings of Jesus are very simple to understand. But Jesus Christ's teachings are not easy to live.

Many, many years ago, when Linda and I started this ministry, God made it very, very clear to both of us that we were not to preach or teach on anything that we haven't lived or are currently living.

We never have and we never will.

I can't help you fly a plane,
because I have never flown one

That would be like me writing a book with a detailed description of how to fly an airplane. Readers wouldn't get very far into the book before they'd be asking me, "Glenn, please tell us what kind of an airplane you fly?"

I'd have to tell you, I don't know how to fly an airplane, any airplane. So, I would immediately loose credibility with you.

So of course it wouldn't be fair for me to tell you, in great detailed description, that God's will for our lives is for us to love unconditionally without giving you my own real life example of unconditional love.

Now, what I'm about to share with you is very personal. It's my own story and it's painful to relate it to you.

61

But I'm telling you this story because it gives glory to God, my Creator, because He loved me enough to show me how to change the way I was living - and to help me change the path I was on.

That's why Linda and I do this. It's the only reason we do this, to give glory to God by letting others know how God wants each of us to live our lives, as part of His great plan.

In 1985, I'd reached a point in my life where I had everything that I was supposed to have to be happy but I was miserable.

One day I went to Linda and I said, "I'm kind of confused about a few things. I just need to get away for a while and sort some things out."

She said, "OK."

I knew there was this little retreat house about three or four miles from where we lived, so I checked into a room and stayed about a week. I didn't go to a retreat, I just checked in. I needed that quiet time to think about what was happening in my life.

So after that week, I called Linda on the phone and told her, "I think I've got one thing figured out."

She said, "I will be right there."

When I walked outside, I saw this beautiful bridge over a little stream. I walked onto this little bridge, watched the stream flowing below, and listened to birds singing in the nearby trees. The whole setting reminded me of a Norman Rockwell painting.

As I stood on this bridge, I saw Linda's car drive up. After she parked it, she saw me there and walked slowly over to the bridge where I was waiting.

Well, she stood three or four feet from me, looked at me lovingly and asked, "How can I help you?"

"Give me a divorce..."

Looking back at her, I said, "You can give me a divorce. I don't love you anymore."

And then I braced myself.

You see I had just told her I didn't love her anymore and I wanted to end our marriage.

I expected her to say the same thing back to me.

My understanding of love at that time was of Eros love.

If I stopped loving her, she would, of course, stop loving me. This was going to be the end of our marriage.

Well, she looked at me with a soft, caring expression that I will never forget.

"Glenn," she said, "I will love you with an everlasting love."

Then she turned around, walked away, got into her car and left.

Now, I have to tell you, that really upset me!

I said, to my startled, disbelieving mind, "What! Didn't that woman hear what I just told her?

How could she ever possibly tell me that she loved me with an everlasting love when I had just told her I wanted to end our marriage, that I didn't love her, that basically I just didn't want anything to do with her anymore?

Well, the next morning, I went down to the local courthouse and I filed for divorce.

She blocked it.

Can you believe that?!

She went to the courthouse and blocked that divorce.

And, then, she called me up. I couldn't believe what she was saying.

"You don't get it do you? We have a sacrament. We stood before God and before our family and our church community and we said we would marry for better or worse," she said. "And, Glenn, this is definitely the worse!"

Well, you can imagine how I reacted to that.

I spent the next 13 months doing everything I could think of to get out of that marriage, everything."

And, all she did was write me little cards.

"I love you."

"I miss you."

"Christina and Kelly miss you. We all miss you. We wish you were here."

You see, I had no defense for that kind of love.

If she had started screaming and hollering at me, fine. I could scream and holler a lot louder than she could.

But, that kind of love, that kind of unconditional love, with no parameters, no boundaries, no limits slowly began to break me down.

Well, because of the choices I had made, I had lost my job, I had lost my wife and - I thought - the love of my two daughters. I was living in my pickup truck, trying to get a grip on all of this.

I had been a regional manager of the largest companies in the United States, I flew all over the country, in first-class seats, stayed in the finest hotels, dined in the finest restaurants - but now I was living in my pickup truck.

You see, I know what it's like to be homeless.

I'll never forget this one night. It was about 2 o'clock in the morning, it was 17 degrees outside, I had an eighth of a tank of gas in my truck and a dollar in my pocket.

About every 15 minutes or so I would start up the truck and keep it running for a while to get warm.

Then, I'd shut it off because if I ran out of gas I'd have to make a choice, either take that dollar in my pocket and buy gas for my truck or use that dollar to get something to eat.

Well, I started up the truck one more time to get warm, turned on the radio and started hitting the station buttons. At the time, I didn't know why I was fooling around with the radio. But now I know it was divine providence.

Aimlessly punching the buttons for different stations and I suddenly found myself listening to Christian music. I can tell you honestly, at that time in my life, I NEVER listened to Christian music.

Then I started listening to the words of that Christian music coming out of those speakers. I know I will never be able to adequately explain to anybody what took place that night in the cab of that truck.

I felt the presence of our almighty sovereign God in a way I had never, ever experienced in my life.

God's spirit filled up the cab of that truck

You see, I know now, that my Lord knew I was going down for the third time. God knew I had no intention of waking up the next morning.

Why bother? I had lost everything. At least I thought I had, so why bother going on?

In every mission that we ever do, I know there is at least one person who walks into that church believing and feeling they're going down for the third time.

And, they don't know why they decided to be at that mission.

I also believe that there will be people reading this book who are at a point where they really don't know exactly why they decided to open these pages.

But, God knows.

Whether attending a mission in a church, or being alone in the privacy of their home with a book, I don't know who they are, and I don't need to know. But I know God is with them, reaching out to them and calling them.

If that person is you, do you honestly believe you have no more love to give to anybody? Do you really feel nobody could possibly love you ever again?

Please remember, when we are at that point in our lives, that is when our Lord Jesus is loving us the most and doing everything He can to reach us, save us and show us the way to new life.

Just 13 months after I stood on that bridge and told my wife, Linda, that I didn't love her anymore, that I wanted a divorce, we stood in a Catholic church and renewed our wedding vows.

I stood at the pulpit and I asked God to forgive me. Then, I asked my wife, Linda, and my two daughters, Christina and Kelly, and my entire faith community to forgive me.

And, they did, just as God forgave me.

If somebody would have told me on our original wedding day that a marriage could be as great as the one we have right now I would have told that person there's never been a marriage created like that.

If somebody would have told me way back then that I could love somebody as much as I love Linda, I would have said I didn't have it in me. And, if somebody would have said to me that Linda could love me as much as she does, I would have said nobody would ever want to love me that way.

I almost threw all of that away.

You see, at some point in every relationship, love no longer is simply a feeling, love becomes a decision.

Once again, as you look at that crucifix, realize that when they nailed Jesus to that cross it did not feel good. When they beat Him, when they scourged Him, when they put the crown of thorns on His head, when they nailed His hands and His feet to that cross, it didn't feel good.

But, our Lord Jesus made a conscious decision of His will to love. I don't believe it was the nails that kept Him on that cross. I believe, with everything in my being, that what kept Jesus on that cross was His love for you and me.

Fortunately for us, when His crucifixion started hurting so much, when His pain became so great, Jesus didn't come down off that cross and cry out to His Father in heaven:

"Father, I'm sorry, this just hurts too much, you're just going to have to figure out a better way."

Jesus hung on that cross for you and for me until He died because He loves us.

Fortunately for me, when the pain of my wanting a divorce became so great for Linda, she didn't say, "I'm sorry, this hurts too much, God, I can't take it any more." Instead, she made a conscious decision of her will and she loved me right back into the kingdom of God.

Wherever we go in this country to bring our missions to new audiences, I always introduce my bride, Linda, as being - next to Jesus - the greatest gift that my father in heaven has ever given me.

Because I believe if it wasn't for the unconditional love of my Lord Jesus and my bride, Linda, I wouldn't be living out the rest of my life telling the story of God's love and the mercy and strength that He's ready to share with each of us - whenever we're ready.

And, I know that God's message is reaching so many people in need because I so often see it happening. For instance, after one of our missions, a woman walked up the aisle afterward to tell me, "Glenn, I've been trying to love that man for 30 years and it's just not working."

Or, a man will come up to me, with tears running down his face, and tell me, "Glenn, my marriage is falling apart, I'm trying to love that woman and it's just not working."

And I will hold up the Bible, look at them and say, "Are you loving them this way?"

And they'll say, "No, I'm not."

That's why there's one Scripture that I always wait to share with people until the end of the second night of our four-day missions.

It's in first Corinthians, Chapter 13, Verse 8.

As you'll see, God has such incredible ability to put so much meaning into so few words.

Now, once again, remember, these are not the words of Deacon Glenn Harmon. These are the words of the Holy Spirit, speaking through the apostle Paul.

In that reading in Corinthians, St. Paul tells us, "Love never fails."

The word that jumps out at me is "never."

God did not say that love will fail for one group of people but another group of people, love will never fail.

God, through St. Paul, said, "Love never fails." That's what He said and what He meant, period!

What is He talking about?

Well, through St. Paul, He's not talking about Eros love, the way most of us have been raised to love. He's not talking about how our society tries to get us to love. Everything that the world is trying to get us to buy into is going to fail. If you try to love somebody in an Eros way, it is eventually going to fail.

What Jesus means when He says "Love never fails" is that agape love, unconditional love, never fails. I believe with everything in me that if husbands and wives would begin to love each other this way there would never be another divorce.

If families would begin to love each other this way there would never be another broken family.

If church communities, rather than tearing each other apart, rather than gossiping about one anther, would begin to come together and love one another this way, you'd be building churches on every street corner and you still couldn't get everybody in who wanted to come.

Our society is in desperate need of this kind of love. Who's going to show them that it works if we, the people who say we are apostles of Jesus Christ, don't do it?

One final thought, remember that earlier, I said that one of the greatest spiritual roadblocks to becoming the person that God wants you to be is "regret."

If you have never been able to love this way, if you have never experienced love this way, please, please do not beat yourself up with regret, shame or guilt. The wonderful thing about Jesus is that we get another shot.

Please, husbands and wives, begin looking at each other like Jesus sees you. Parents, children, grandchildren, faith communities, please learn to love this way.

Our families, our churches, our society are in great need of that kind of love.

Our Prayer for God's Love

In the name of the Father and the Son and the Holy Spirit, we pray.

Lord, we thank you for being with us in moments like this, whether at a mission or reading the pages of this book.

We thank you, Lord, for giving us your word and for loving us the way that you do. Lord, instill in us the desire, the gift of your love, that we will be willing to make the choice that love is your will for our lives, that we will begin to act on it with every breath and every action that we do.

We thank you, Lord Jesus, for dying on the cross for us, for your unconditional mercy in spite of who we are and what we do every day.

Lord, please lift us up with your power and protect us with your love.

We ask all of these things in the name of our Almighty Father God, and your Son, our Lord and our Savior, Jesus Christ.

Amen.

A Call To Action

1. What is the deepest desire of your heart right now? Have you shared that desire with God in prayer?

2. Have you ever asked our Lord to reveal His will for your life?

3. What did you think, and how did you feel, when I said that God's will for your life is to love?

4. Right now, are you extending Eros or agape love to those important people in your life? What action can you take to live a more agape life?

5. At this moment, who is the hardest person for you to love? Why?

6. What specific actions can you take to love that person in the way that God wants you to love them?

7. What was your reaction when you realized how much God loves you each day of your life?

Chapter 3

Walk By Faith

Linda Harmon

Learning to walk by faith is important to each one of us because God is not only our Creator but also our partner in helping us grow in our Christian faith.

You can be sure God is present with us each day. He wants to bless us abundantly, right where we are, no matter what circumstance we are in at the time.

If we approach each day with expectant faith, we can believe God will touch us and walk with us in a very personal and real way.

I want to share with you my story of learning to walk by faith.

The experience of sharing our faith is one definition of Evangelization. When we tell others how God has touched our life, they are encouraged and helped to deepen their own spiritual life. We can always use each others' help.

As Glenn shared in the last chapter, our family has been through some spiritually challenging times.

God has led us through those challenges to a place of calm, loving discipleship with Him.

Glenn and I have both become modern-day apostles of Jesus to help others benefit from our experiences, and better understand God and His love for each of us.

We have learned the true value of living our lives by walking in the faith of our Lord, Jesus Christ. Faith and love have made all the difference in our lives even as we've faced challenges, disappointments and emotional stress in so many ways.

My own journey of faith is not the result of anything I have done for God but rather what God has done for me.

It's about how He has and how He continues to rescue and heal me every day. This is the story of my spiritual walk with Jesus, my story of God's great love for me.

I'll be describing a lot of things that have touched my life, things like how God healed me of the effects of verbal, physical and sexual abuse that happened to me when I was a child.

I'll share about living with an alcoholic parent in a dysfunctional home and how I found out, as an adult, that I had been adopted as a baby.

I'll be sharing about the time that my husband told me that he wanted a divorce. And, I'll share with you what God did to heal our lives and our marriage.

I'll describe some of my trials as a parent and how I made it through so many challenges when one of my children was involved with alcohol and drug abuse.

And, I'll share with you how I handled my mother's death and my feelings of pain, fear, worry, loneliness, rejection, abandonment and my experience of being broken and wounded physically, emotionally and spiritually.

But, most importantly, I'll tell you how God, in His unconditional love and mercy for me, continues to restore and heal me every day.

We all live out the pascal mysteries - those birth, suffering, dying and resurrection moments. However, so many of us just want those resurrection moments. We don't want the suffering and the dying moments.

But, that's just not the way life is.

All people live the pascal mystery, but as Christians, we see that Jesus, through His example, shows us the way to walk through the suffering and the dying moments of life. He has shown us the way, and given us the ability to walk with a peace that is beyond all understanding.

That sounds absurd to the world. But God wants His children to go through life with a joy, a peace and a freedom that is beyond all understanding. He has shown us the way to walk by faith and not by sight.

My story of faith began when I was a very young girl, about the age of four or five. I was sexually abused by a neighbor for some time. After the police came and took a report we never talked about it again in my family.

I remember a girl on the school playground telling me that I made a man go to jail because I was bad and nasty. I remember feelings of guilt and shame that I carried with me for many years.

Several years ago, in prayer, the Lord brought the memory of all of this to my mind and He showed me that I needed to forgive that neighbor. I needed to be healed of all of my shame, guilt, anger and pain. God showed me that it was a burden that I had been carrying around for years and He wanted to set me free.

I know that there are people reading this book who have been sexually abused. Some of you have been healed. Praise God! Some of you are still carrying around the burden of what happened to you. Some of you still carry that pain, guilt, shame and anger. You have not released it yet, and allowed God to heal you.

With God's help, I invite you to let it go, too.

God reminded me that when Jesus went to the cross, and died for us, He did that for all sins, everyone's sins. When Jesus died, He paid the price with His life for the sin that was done against me and for the sin that was done against you. Jesus paid the price in full with His life.

God also reminded me that I was still the one in bondage because I had never forgiven this man.

God was asking me to forgive him so that I could walk in freedom and peace and be free from all of those chains of the past that were holding me in bondage.

Forgiveness does not excuse or condone the offense. Forgiveness is to act and do God's will in our life. So, I prayed to God for strength and I forgave this man. Then I asked God to heal me and I asked God to heal him. I made a conscious and deliberate decision to forgive, despite how I felt.

As I prayed, I felt God's loving, healing power. I felt like a little child again, and I visualized myself climbing up into a loving father's lap. He held me and He comforted me. I know God the Father now as Abba, as my Daddy. As I was allowing myself to be loved by Abba, I knew then that God loved this man just as much as He loved me, that His love and His mercy were for both of us.

With God's grace, and my decision to yield my will and my memories of this event to the will of God, He healed me of that pain, anger and shame which I had unconsciously held on to for so many years. This takes time but forgiveness is a decision that needs to be made.

For those reading this who still feel that pain of unforgiveness in your lives, I invite you today to ask God to come into your hearts to heal and restore you like He did for me.

God is just waiting for your decision and your willingness to let go. Sometimes it takes time for the feelings of pain and hurt to pass and this is not a one-time action.

When I was growing up, my father was in the Navy, so we moved around a lot. By the time I was 18 years old we had lived in 20 different cities. I had a hard time feeling like I really belonged anywhere. And it was always difficult trying to make new friends.

My parents only went to church on Easter and Christmas, if that. But, if someone invited my sisters and me to go to church we went along. They were all different churches and different denominations.

In the sixth grade, I fell in love with Jesus. We had learned the story of the Good Shepherd and I memorized the 23rd Psalm, which really touched my heart.

Jesus says, in Luke 15:4-7, "Who among you, if he owns 100 sheep, and loses one of them, does not leave the 99 and search for the lost one until he finds it? And, when he finds it, he puts it on his shoulders in jubilation and once he arrives home he invites his friends and his neighbors and says to them, 'Rejoice with me, because I have found my lost sheep.' I tell you there will likewise be more joy in heaven over one repentant sinner than over 99 righteous people who have no need to repent."

I remember being so amazed that Jesus, as the Good Shepherd, would leave that flock of 99 and go after that one lost sheep. Because even at that young age I already felt like I was lost and alone - a lost sheep.

Are there times in your life when you feel lost and alone?

I think one of the reasons I felt so alone and scared was the fact that my father was an alcoholic.

It was very hard growing up in a dysfunctional home. Some of you reading this know what I'm talking about.

I knew my father loved us very much. And, I knew he could be very loving and wonderful. I had some great memories of our family when I was a child.

But, as his drinking got worse, so did his verbal abuse.

Because of his personality, and his Navy background, he liked to run a tight ship, even at home. He could be a very hard man at times.

My mother, on the other hand, was loving, gentle, friendly and kind. But, she had no rules at all.

When my dad was out to sea for nine to 13 months at a time, we lived our lives without conflict and my mother was very lenient.

But when my dad came home, everything would change. My sisters and I grew up with such verbal abuse that many times dad's words would bring us all to tears, even my mother.

I especially hated dinner time on my dad's day off because he'd be drinking all day long. It seemed to be the perfect time for him to start picking on all of us for the things that we didn't do right. Because I was the oldest, it seemed I was most often the one who was in trouble.

I never knew when I'd be sent to my room from the dinner table because I hadn't eaten my dinner the way that he wanted. He put food on our plate at 3, 6 and 9 o'clock and I had to make sure I ate my food clockwise or it would set him off into a rage.

Because of things like that, I grew up with very little confidence. I had low self-esteem.

Still, as a child, I loved my dad, and I loved him as an adult, until the day he died. And, he knew it. When I was a child I'd go fishing with him and I tried to be a tomboy because he said he always wanted a son.

My dad's drinking and abuse got worse as I got older. Later, while I was in college, my dad got physically abusive with me.

My parents separated and later they got a divorce. Even then, I would try so hard to please my dad but I always fell short. I think I felt the same way about God. I wanted to be good and I wanted to please God but I knew so often that I fell short.

I thought if only I just tried a little harder, then He'd love me.

Do you sometimes feel like you fall short with God? Do you feel that if only you could just try a little harder then God would love you, too?

Is your idea of God sometimes like that parent who constantly reminds you of how bad you are and how much you have failed?

Do you see God as someone who keeps score and so you feel you can never do enough good to outweigh all the bad that you do? I think many people have low self-esteem and low self-worth anyway. And I believe there are people reading this book who have grown up with verbal and physical abuse, far worse than I can imagine.

I also believe that some of you have been abused for so long that you don't believe you have or are anything of value.

But, you know what?

That's just not true.

God says, in Isaiah 43:4, that "you are precious in my eyes and glorious because I love you."

That is such an awesome thought. Even after all these years, I know I haven't grasped the reality of that truth completely.

Just think, God said that we, His children, are precious to Him and He loves us.

I believe that if we could really absorb what that means, none of us, none of us, would ever have a low self-esteem problem again.

We would all face this world everyday in confidence. We would say to others, "Do to me whatever you want. It doesn't matter to me what you think, because I am precious and glorious to my God, and He loves me."

Have you ever felt - or been made to feel - you aren't precious and loved? Do you know this is a lie that Satan tries to tell us all the time? It's a lie because God says you are precious and glorious in His sight. You are loved by your Creator, your God.

Who are you going to believe, Satan or God?

You don't have to do a thing to earn God's love. He just loves you. He created you just the way you are and He knows everything about you, and me, and it doesn't matter.

God just loves you.

God can heal anything. That includes any pain, any situations or anything you have to deal with. God wants us to invite Him into the broken, wounded areas of our lives and accept His healing love and mercy.

But, He will require us to extend love and forgiveness to our enemies, those who have hurt us.

Now, I have forgiven my father, for his sickness and for his sins against me, and I love my dad very much.

Look at your own life. Who is your enemy? Who has hurt you the most?

God is asking you to extend forgiveness to those who have hurt you so you can be healed and free.

I'd like to share with you now a little bit about my young adult years and my married life.

I met my husband Glenn in college. He was a Catholic who loved God and his church very much.

And I wanted what he had, so I became Catholic. We were married in the church in April of 1970. This year, as I write these words in 2014, we have been married for 44 years.

Right after our oldest daughter, Christina, was born I found out, in a very painful way, that I had been adopted as a baby.

I had no idea that I had been adopted and it came as quite a shock to me. I felt so much pain. I felt rejected, unwanted and wounded by my birth mother giving me up for adoption.

Because I was adopted, I wondered if that was why I always felt a lack of belonging in my family, even though I was much loved by my parents. But, God helped me to recall the passage from the Bible in Isaiah 49:14-15, when God said, "Even should a mother forget her child, I will never forget you."

Now, some of you reading about this experience may be adopted, too. And, you may feel rejected by your mother or feel abandoned or go through times when you feel like you just don't belong. Realize that all of us, at one time or another, feel unwanted and rejected, for many reasons.

But, God reminded me, and He reminds you, that there are no orphans in God's family. We all belong to Him. We are all adopted and heirs to God Himself.

God showed me that instead of feeling rejection, I needed to pray for my biological parents and let go of the feelings that I had of being an unwanted child.

I especially prayed for my mother and I asked God to relieve her of any guilt and pain that she might have had, or maybe she still has today - to give her His peace.

In prayer, God asked me to think of her and what pain she must have gone through as a young, unwed mother, and the scandal she must have suffered in making that kind of decision.

In Colossians 3:15 the Bible says, "Christ's peace must reign in your heart since, as members of the one body, we have been called to that peace. Dedicate yourself to thankfulness."

I started doing just that. I prayed and I thanked my mother for making that difficult choice to have me and to give me away for adoption, rather than having an abortion.

God flooded my heart with mercy and compassion for my biological parents and He gave me a new appreciation for my adoptive parents.

If we will dedicate ourselves to thankfulness, it will become very difficult to feel bad about our own situation. We need to keep an attitude of gratitude and then we will more readily see how God is working in our lives and how much He does love us.

After Glenn and I had been married for several years, we started a disillusionment phase in our relationship.

We had two small children who were only 13 months apart. We had really bad money problems, and we got all caught up in our jobs, kids and just all the things that were going on. We stopped going to church and we stopped caring for one another. We had no life together and no love for one another.

I remember lying in bed together for several nights and thinking how amazing it is that two people could be in the same bed, only inches apart, but feel like the Grand Canyon was between us.

Have you ever felt that way in your marriage?

78

Did you ever feel like your marriage was slowly dying and yet you felt there was nothing you could do about it?

Through God's love and mercy we did have a resurrection moment in our marriage. My best friend encouraged us to make a Marriage Encounter weekend, where God showed us that we have a Sacrament and that marriage was our vocation in life.

At that moment we fell in love with each other, with our God and with our church all over again. Actually, love is a decision, not a feeling.

We went back to our church and it seemed we just couldn't do enough. We were a team couple for Marriage Encounter; we were working in youth ministry; we were members of the choir and involved in anything else that needed to be done. We attended a Life in the Spirit seminar and God turned up the flame of desire for us to serve.

We were so happy as a family.

Glenn and I attended a week-long school of Evangelization and we got even more excited about working for the Lord.

We heard so many wonderful things, such as learning that we were called to be apostles and that we had a job to do today in the church, just like Peter and Paul did back in the time of Jesus.

After that school, Glenn quit his job. We decided that we both wanted to serve the Lord full time.

And then, through unbelievable acts of God that we call Godcidentals, not coincidentals, Glenn became the director of youth ministry for the Diocese of Boise, Idaho. Also, I became a pastoral associate for our parish and a leader for a women's prayer group.

Life was just great!

...for a couple of years.

But, as time passed, we got all caught up in doing our own thing again.

Glenn's territory was the entire state of Idaho, all 86,000 square miles. So he was always gone again, especially nights and weekends.

We started growing apart - again.

That was also a time when I started to realize that it was quite possible to do Godly work without God being at the center of all of it. You can fool yourself and others for a short amount of time, but the truth will come forth.

Our schedules were so full that we were left with no time to spend with each other.

Then, one day, out of the blue, Glenn told me that he wanted a divorce and that he didn't love me anymore. I had feelings of shock, disbelief, doubt, fear, rejection, loneliness, pain and complete abandonment.

I felt like a hole had just been ripped out from the center of me and my entire life was caving in around me. I questioned how God could have let that happen.

Some of you, I'm sure, know exactly what I'm talking about. Others may not know those feelings that come from a word like "divorce." But certainly other devastating things may have occurred in your life that - like the reality of the word divorce - made you question God, asking Him, "God, how could you let something like this happen to me or to my family?"

You, like me, at some point in your life, may have experienced more pain than you ever could have imagined and wondered how you could handle that situation.

I'd like to share how God helped me through this time of devastation.

My hope is that my experiences of the power of God in the midst of this devastation might be of use to you now or that you might keep it in your heart and use it for a later time in your life.

Remember, we all live the paschal mystery: birth, suffering, dying and resurrection. God gave me some powerful scriptures and insight into how to apply them.

He also sent me a few strong prayer warriors to help me in this battle. Yes, it was a battle, because I knew this was a war. My enemy, however, was Satan and his evil spirit of divorce. I knew it wasn't Glenn.

God showed me that I had to stand and face the enemy of divorce, not only for me but for my two girls and for my grandchildren. You see, I came from a long line of divorces in my family. My own mother and father, as well as each of their mothers and fathers had gotten divorces or separations.

I knew this chain of divorce just had to be broken in my family line.

The first scripture God gave me was Isaiah 58:9, "You shall call and the Lord will answer. You shall cry for help and He will say, 'Here I am.'"

I did call for help and God assured me He was with me and that I wasn't alone in this battle. He was there.

So whatever battle you're going through, please know that you are not in it alone. God is with you. You can depend on the Lord. I felt God's assurance that Glenn and I had a Sacramental union and that we would get through this and be healed.

Now I didn't know how God could make this happen, because at that time I didn't even like Glenn any more, much less love him. I kept asking God, "What is your will in this matter?" And then I knew, beyond a shadow of a doubt, that it was God's will for us to stay together. We were a Sacrament!

I told God I didn't know how He would work it out but that I would do my part to remain faithful to our marriage.

Are there areas in your life that you are wondering how God will help you work it out? It looks impossible in the natural world!

That's why God tells us to walk by faith and not by sight.

We are called to do our part in the battle, which means praying and not giving up, for the battle belongs to the Lord. We aren't supposed to believe what we see in the natural world. We are supposed to believe what God says.

God led me to the most wonderful scripture and insight into its meaning, and I'd like to share it with you. You can apply it right now to so many situations in your life, and always hold on to it for later occasions. God urged me to read St. Paul's letter to the Philippians, 4:4-9.

"Rejoice in the Lord, always, I say again, rejoice. Everyone should see how unselfish you are. The Lord is near. Dismiss all anxiety from your mind. Present your needs to God in all forms of prayer and petition, full of gratitude. Then, God's peace, which is beyond all understanding, will stand guard over your heart and mind in Christ Jesus."

Finally, St. Paul writes, "Your thoughts should be wholly directed to all that is true, all that deserves respect, all that is honest, pure, admirable, decent, virtuous, and worthy of praise. Live according to what you have learned and accepted, what you have heard me say and seen me do. Then will the God of Peace be with you."

After reading that passage, I asked God if He was sure about leading me to this scripture. As I continued to pray, He led me to understand and believe that Bible passage in my heart and to see how it applied to my situation. Can you believe this for you and your situation?

Now the first thing it says to do is rejoice. It's so important that God says it again, "I say again, rejoice!"

That's a pretty tough order when all you feel like doing is crying and getting angry.

But, one of the first things I realized was that I would not get through this operating on a "feeling" level. I had to follow God's direction.

So that was my first lesson, not to act or react on my feelings, which changed moment by moment. But to make a conscious and deliberate decision to be obedient to the will of God.

Now some of God's scripture direction was, for a long time, puzzling to me, particularly the passage that said, "Everyone should see how unselfish you are."

Part of that scripture may puzzle you, as it puzzled me. I was months into this journey before I really understood the meaning of, "Everyone should see how unselfish you are."

I prayed this scripture passage daily, sometimes ten times a day, to get through those emotionally hard times.

What I came to understand is that when you don't act according to your feelings, but instead make your decisions in obedience to God's will despite your feelings, this is a very unselfish act.

I learned the truth of what Jesus means in scripture when He says, "God is with you. Know that you are not in this battle alone. He is right by your side." The next line says, "Dismiss all anxiety from your mind."

What jumped out at me was the word, "all."

He didn't say you could hold onto some of your anxiety. Jesus said "all anxiety."

It was not just a suggestion, it was more like a command, to not allow any anxiety into your mind.

That was very difficult for me because my mother was a worrier, so I saw that constantly as I was growing up. She seemed to feel that she wasn't doing a good job as a mother unless she was worrying.

And that example influenced my own life.

Great news for worriers!
Become a great warrior - for God!

Well, I have some great news for you if you are a good worrier. Instead, you can be a great warrior for the Lord.

Worriers have their focus on how big their problem is. What you really need to focus on is how big your God is. God is looking for warriors to do battle for His kingdom - not worriers!

Next, Jesus said, "Present your needs to God in every form of prayer and in petitions full of gratitude."

I asked God how in the world can I do that?

Well, God showed me that to present your needs to Him full of gratitude means to see the situation as already resolved, in God's way, a way that would give Him the glory.

And I knew that it would give God glory to heal and restore our sacrament of marriage.

So, as I continued praying all those months, I began believing that God would do it. I began to see with eyes of faith and not with eyes of sight.

That was certainly not following my feelings, because everything around me looked absolutely hopeless. It looked like our marriage was already dead.

The next line of scripture says, "God's own peace, which is beyond all understanding, will stand guard over your heart and your mind in Christ Jesus."

Then, God showed me what I like to refer to as my "glory bubble."

Every time Glenn and I would get together, a lot of painful and hurtful things were being said.

So what I did was to visualize myself inside this protective bubble, covered and protected by God from head to toe, inside my "glory bubble."

I knew that if words were said to hurt me that I would let them come into my heart and my mind and that later on I would have to work at releasing that pain and releasing those feelings of unforgiveness.

So each time we met and hurtful things were said, I just placed myself inside this glory bubble, imagining it covered me from the top of my head to the tips of my toes. It was truly a bubble of protection. The words would just hit it and slide right off. That way, I never took them into my heart.

This was a great help to me. I know, of course, that it must have infuriated Satan, because he wanted me to develop a hard heart and live with a lot of angry thoughts.

Instead, I was letting God's peace guard my heart and my mind.

Now, I am not telling you that this was easy. I still felt the pain but those hurtful words stirred up inside of me such a Godly righteousness, which allowed me to stand and face this enemy called divorce and strengthened me in the battle.

The next line of that scripture says "your thoughts should be wholly" - not partially, mind you - but "wholly directed to all that is true, all that deserves respect, all that is honest, pure, admirable, decent, virtuous and worthy of praise."

You know, that just doesn't leave much room for stinking thinking. There's only room for those victorious thoughts, not those "what if" thoughts, which is the Devil's way of making us wallow in worry, doubt and fear.

Fear, I think, is the really big one to avoid because, you know, battles like this are waged in our minds, so what we think about really matters. Our thoughts will either help us or hurt us.

In Romans 12:2, Christ tells us that we must renew our minds and put on the mind of Christ. Then scripture says, in Philippians 4:9, "Live according to what you have learned and accepted, what you have heard me say and seen me do."

I've learned and accepted that God is more powerful than Satan.

You know what?

We can win these spiritual battles. We will win. Victory will be ours, with God's help.

Jesus meant for me to believe and live my life as though my marriage was already healed.

Either God is God or He is not.

The promises of His word are either true or they are not. The last line of that scripture says, "Then will the God of peace be with you." God promises us peace. And peace is what we need so badly when we're in the middle of a battle.

God's peace helped me get through every single day of pain.

Have you gone through, or are you currently going through, a devastating battle that is like a crucifixion in your life?

When you pray to God for help, remember that nothing, absolutely nothing, is too great for God to handle.

And, remember, too, that God wants to help us. We are His children. He created us.

Someone once wrote, "God never tires of helping us. We are the ones who tire of asking for God's help."

Apply these messages of Philippians 4:4-9 to whatever you're going through, and let God's peace be with you. The experiences Glenn and I lived through, with God's help, prove that God and His scriptures can help you, too.

After all of our trials and tribulations, 13 months to the day after Glenn asked for a divorce, God showed us His mercy and compassion by restoring our broken marriage.

We look at that as truly a resurrection moment in our marriage.

Finally, after all of the months of heartache, pain and battle, Glenn and I renewed our marriage vows before hundreds of friends and family. Glenn stood at the pulpit that day and asked for my forgiveness and the forgiveness of our daughters, our community and our God.

Again, God in His mercy was creating something new between us. He wasn't just fixing up our old marriage, He was making our marriage new and better than ever before.

I learned so much from this experience.

I learned that I could love more than I ever imagined I could, because Jesus taught me to love, not with my own love, but with His love.

Our own love comes to an end. But the love of Jesus never ends, never runs out. As children of God we are allowed the privilege of tapping into and using the love of Jesus, through the Holy Spirit.

When we live our lives by the guidance of the Holy Spirit, we tap into the love of Jesus. We are able to love with that unconditional and limitless love of God, our Father, not with just our own love, which is very conditional and has its limits.

But, unfortunately, Glenn sought forgiveness from everyone except himself.

You know, sometimes we are the hardest person to forgive.

Have you found that true in your life? I have certainly found it true in mine.

At this point, although our marriage was saved and blessed, Glenn felt so unworthy to serve God and His church that we left ministry work. We moved back to San Diego and Glenn went back to the corporate world.

During the next couple of years, our youngest daughter began having a lot of trouble in school. Then she got involved with the wrong group of friends. She became angry and rebellious and soon was out of control.

We just tried everything to reach her. We tried loving her more, finding counseling, apply more discipline but nothing seemed to work. She was obviously on a downhill spiral. It was really getting worse and worse. She started running away from home, and even tried to commit suicide.

Of course, we felt so helpless.

Have you ever felt totally helpless when it came to your children and their lives?

You look at them and their actions and you're just at a loss about what to do?

Well, next came one of the hardest decisions we ever had to make. We admitted her into a rehab hospital - and left her there. She hated us for doing that and she wasn't willing to cooperate for a long time.

All Glenn and I could do was pray.

Fortunately, our faith community was there for us. We had a lot of friends supporting us and we experienced their prayers holding us together.

Have you ever experienced being connected to community and feeling their love and the support of their prayers holding you together? That's why we all need to be connected.

You see, God never intended for us to walk this earthly walk alone. We are on this journey together because we are the Church. Slowly, over time, through the grace of God, she started her healing process.

Today, she is a strong and wonderful person. She is now married and has a beautiful daughter, and I know that she knows and loves God. I'm standing in the gap for her by praying every single day.

Is there a child or grandchild you are standing in the gap for today?

Please pray Isaiah 43:5-6, which says, "Fear not, for I am with you. From the East I will bring back your descendants and from the West I will gather you. I will say to the North, give them up, and to the South, hold not back. Bring back my sons from afar and my daughters from the ends of the Earth."

You know God has them covered, from the north, east, west and south, even from the ends of the Earth. God will bring back our children and our grandchildren. That is His promise. That's not my promise.

Do you know that prayer is the most important thing that we can do?

That's our part in the battle. Walk by faith, not by sight. We should never underestimate the power of persistent prayer.

We can move past all that pain and enter into the throne room of grace and lay our petitions before God, full of gratitude.

Our prayers need to be bold and full of hope. We need to ask Jesus to help us increase our faith and believe that He can and will heal and restore. But, we don't need to know how He's going to do it.

For me, if I knew God's plan, I'd probably try to step in, take over and botch it all up.

We need to make an act of faith, to choose to believe and then act as though God has already done it. Even though we might not be able to see how, we must be able to see the situation with eyes of faith.

Remember that Hebrews 11:1-2 says, "Faith is confident assurance concerning what we hope for and conviction about things we do not see."

What are you hoping for today? What do you not see that you need to believe? Believe that God is working to resolve your problem in a way that will give Him glory. God wants us to have, and live with, His Joy, according to John 15:11.

Also, Hebrews 11:6 says, "Without faith it is impossible to please God." Do you want to please God? I know that I do. So operate in faith.

Does the thought of death make you fearful?

Now there is just one other topic that I would like to touch on.

That topic is death.

I used to be so fearful of death that I could hardly talk about it without crying.

In September 1992, my mother died suddenly, at the age of 66. It was a real shock to me. We were very close. I think sometimes you just don't know how much you really love someone until they're gone.

I guess I thought that we had many, many more years to share our lives and our love together. But you know, we just never know when it's our time, or the time for a loved one, to go home to be with the Lord.

So, we need to make every day count and not take each other for granted. We need to enjoy and treasure those special, wonderful people that God has placed in our lives.

We need to remember to make every single day count. We must live in the present moment. Yesterday is gone, and no matter how hard we try, we cannot enter into tomorrow. God is eternal. God always has been, is now and always will be. We can only live in the present moment so "now" is the only time we have.

If we want to love, the only time that we have to love is now. If we want to trust, hope, forgive, have joy and peace, the only time we can do it is now.

If you want to pray and stand in the gap for someone, or if you want to serve God with all your heart, the only time you can do it is now.

My faith and my belief is that my mother is in heaven, face to face with God. That thought gives me much joy and hope and has taken my fear away. So love today all of those special people that God has placed in your life.

Our marriage was healed and our family restored. Glenn was back in the fast lane of the corporate world. However, I sensed that my husband was wrestling with God. There was a hole inside of him that money, power, recognition and authority would not fill.

No matter what title the world had given him, Glenn still knew that his true identity was an apostle of the Lord Jesus Christ.

There was a still, small voice within him that kept saying, "I want you." Glenn knew it was the voice of the Holy Spirit, but he felt he was unworthy to serve the Lord and His church because of his past failures.

Over time, God reminded Glenn of how St. Peter had denied Christ three times, how St. Thomas had doubted that Jesus had truly risen from the dead. In spite of those failures, our Lord called these men to proclaim the Gospel to the ends of the world.

After many years of healing, prayer, discernment, dialogue and guidance by the Holy Spirit, we decided to be obedient to the Lord's call. We turned our backs on the "Gospel of the World" and made the choice to live for the "Gospel of Christ.:

It has been an amazing journey so far. Jesus keeps saying, "Follow me!" And we keep saying, "Yes, Lord." Together, we serve an amazing, awesome and mighty God!

Glenn and I have now been in full-time ministry since July 1992. And, like every other aspect of our lives, our walk in this ministry has reflected Christ's pascal mystery - the birth, suffering, dying and wonderful resurrection moments.

We travel the country doing missions, retreats and days of renewal. We are a living witness to the sacrament of marriage, showing others how God can and will use all things for good for those who love the Lord.

You know, we all try and fail so many times to live our lives by giving God the glory, but all God asks of us is to try.

He asks for our willingness to walk by faith rather than by sight.

What I'm learning every day is that I need to grow in faith and surrender everything to the Lord. My safety, my security, my finances and my family. I have to trust and give them all to the Lord. Without Jesus being at the center of everything, and the guidance of the Holy Spirit, it is all in vain.

You know, God is either God or He's not. His promises are either true for us or they're not. And, the Bible is either the greatest story that's ever been told or it's the greatest lie that's ever been written. It's either one or the other, it cannot be both.

What is it for you today?

For me, it's following the true, living word of God.

What I'm developing in my life is a real sense of how desperate this world is for a Savior and how important my role - and your role - is in bringing that message to the world.

You know, we live in a time of evil. Almost everything society professes goes completely against the values and the principles of God.

People are desperate for the mercy, compassion and the message of God. We need to hear and live the good news, that there is a Savior for all of us and His name is Jesus, the Good Shepherd who always cares enough to go after His lost sheep.

He's sending us. We are the hands and the feet of Jesus. He's sending us with a message of love and forgiveness, not just with our words but also with our actions.

Jesus calls us to love our enemies, to do good to those who hate us, to bless those who curse us and to pray for those who mistreat us.

Read Luke 6:27-28. In the "Our Father,' which is the prayer that Jesus wanted us to know, we say, "Forgive us our trespasses as we forgive those who trespass against us."

I believe that it's unforgiveness that keeps us in bondage. It steals our joy, our peace and our freedom. God says, "Know the truth and the truth will set you free." What pain or bondage in your life do you need to be set free?

God has shown me in my life, over and over again, that I need to forgive. That's a gift I give to myself as well as to the one who hurt me. God always gives us a choice. He says, in Deuteronomy 30:19, "Choose this day the way of life or death."

God gives us the way. God sent His own son, Jesus, to be our model, to show us that the right way to live is to embrace our own cross and be guided by God's word.

Whether we are a believer or not, we all have crosses in our lives to bear. But Jesus promises us that if we will pick up our cross and carry it to the Father, and lean on Him and His truth, then we will be set free.

Now, this is our choice: to surrender our will to the Father. And, when we do this, God will change our Good Friday into Easter joy. We will experience the resurrection even though that joy is seen as an absurdity to the world.

If we choose not to forgive, we are sentencing ourselves to a lifetime of pain and despair. God doesn't want this for His children. He gave us a way to walk in peace.

God said, "I have come to give you life, and to give it to you abundantly."

But, fear keeps us from that abundant living. F. E. A. R., meaning: False Evidence Appearing Real. I've heard this for many years. This is the lie that Satan tries to tell us and we buy into it all the time.

When I was fearful and I prayed, God showed me a choice, He showed me what faith is - F.A.I.T.H, Father Affirming my Inheritance of Truth and Hope.

Faith, like grace, is a gift from God.

A measure of faith is given to each one of us. We can either bury it and forget about it, and drift farther from our Creator, or we can use it and see our faith develop and grow, with God's help. As children of God we are called to exercise our faith so that it grows, takes over and fills us so doubt and fear and worry and anxiety will have no room in our lives.

Over and over again, in scripture, God tells us, His children, do not be afraid. I've discovered that fear isn't a lack of believing.

Fear is believing in the wrong thing.

It's believing in the natural realm, in what we see with our sight. It's listening and believing what Satan wants to tell us.

But faith, on the other hand, is believing what God says and shows us.

Remember, F.A.I.T.H. means our Father Affirming our Inheritance of Truth and Hope.

It is our inheritance because we are "born again" children of God, and we are His heirs to the kingdom. It is the truth that sets us free.

It is our hope that gives us the ability to walk in the suffering, dying moments of our life knowing, deep in our hearts, that God is in charge and He will turn all of our sorrows into resurrection moments.

He is who He says He is.

God's promises are true, for you and for me.

Remember, God has told us that you are precious and glorious in His eyes and He loves you.

I love you, too.

May God bless you always.

Our Closing Prayer

Heavenly Father, you know my heart. You are aware of the joy, hurt and pain that it holds. I want to walk and grow in my faith. Help me to surrender any concern, worry, anxiety or fear that I may have deep within me.

I want to be a mighty warrior for you and not a worrier. I can only do this with your grace. Help me to forgive myself or anyone who has hurt me. Grant me the abundant life that you want for me and have promised for me.

Lord, I ask and I receive at this moment your peace, hope, love and joy. I ask all these desires of my heart in and through the precious and holy name of my Lord and Savior, Jesus Christ.

Amen.

A Call to Action

1. In what areas of my life do I desire and need more faith?

2. What are the steps I can take to grow in faith in this area?

3. Do I need to give the gift of forgiveness to myself or to anyone else in my life? If my answer is "Yes," am I you willing to ask for God's grace to act?

4. What are the specific steps I can make to move myself from living with the "chains" of unforgiveness to the freedom of forgiveness?

Chapter 4

A Decision of the Will

You might very well finish this chapter as a new person, liberated from past decisions, past views or past regrets.

However, for many readers it may be a chapter filled with words that will make you squirm in your chair, because this is a very challenging topic.

You are going to be introduced to what I call a spiritual pathway, a pathway that will take you from unforgiveness to forgiveness and then to reconciliation.

I'm talking about an epidemic we have in our world that is affecting how many of us live our lives, an epidemic of unforgiveness.

Unforgiveness is literally ripping our country's societies apart.

Six out of 10 marriages in this country end in divorce today, because one or both people refuse to forgive one another. It's destroying families, it's ripping apart church communities.

Sadly, this is a topic we don't think about often or spend much time talking about. We tend to ignore our unforgiveness.

How many times during a regular day, either at work, or school, or at home, have you said during your conversations with people, "Oh, by the way, I'm not sure you know this but I've been holding unforgiveness against five people in my life."

Of course, you wouldn't do that.

My point is that we just don't talk about this stuff. And, because we don't talk about it, we don't think about it. Because we don't think about it or talk about it we don't do anything about it.

Yet, many people live their entire lives bound in these chains of unforgiveness because they are riddled throughout their souls with unforgiveness.

At our mission presentations, I usually begin our focus on unforgiveness with a prayer that you can offer, too, as you begin reading this chapter. I ask our merciful Father to give us His mercy, grace and forgiveness in our times of need.

And, I ask God to bring all of us freedom from being shackled by feelings of resentment or unforgiveness.

Then, I ask God to give each of us a new heart to love Him, so that our lives will reflect the image of His son, Jesus, our Savior.

And, I ask God to help the people of the world see the glory of His Son revealed and that He truly is the one that God has sent to save us.

In the Catholic Church, forgiveness specifically focuses on reconciliation, a big word that simply means re-establishing healthful, loving, forgiving relationships, between ourselves and our God and between ourselves and other people.

Our Catholic Church teaches us that when our Lord, Jesus Christ, went to the cross for us 2,000 years ago He re-established, re-connected that broken relationship between all of humanity and God, our Father.

If that same Jesus Christ was to shine His Gospel on every relationship any of us have in our lives, past or present, would any of those relationships be in need of reconciliation?

Are you holding any anger, resentment, bitterness or unforgiveness against anybody in your life, past or present? Please be honest with yourself and specific!

Maybe you're holding unforgiveness against a group of people, or a certain situation that has taken place in your life.

This is when you need to call on the Holy Spirit to give you the grace to forgive.

Linda and I always include this topic in our missions for three primary reasons.

The first is that I discovered in a very powerful way, a number of years ago, my difficulty - in fact, my unwillingness - to forgive certain people in my life.

It all became clear to me one Sunday morning at Mass.

When it was time for the Lord's prayer (Matthew 6:9-13), we all stood up, and I took the hand of the person on the right of me and the person on the left of me. Then we began to say the prayer that Jesus taught us to pray, the same prayer He gave to his apostles when they asked Him how they should pray.

I don't know if you're like me in this particular way, but I've probably said the Lord's prayer tens of thousands of times in my life.

So when I know a prayer that well, when I have memorized it so many years ago, sometimes I'm not consciously thinking of what those words really, really mean. I'm not thinking about the real, root meaning of that prayer. On that particular Sunday morning, at that particular Mass, I soon discovered that God was going to make sure that I understood what that prayer really means.

When we came to the part that said, "Lord, forgive me my trespasses," I became very much aware that what I was saying was asking God to forgive me for anything and everything that I had ever done to hurt Him or anyone else in my life.

And that reminded me very clearly that I had done some very heavy duty things to hurt God and many people in my life. Yet, I was asking God to forgive me, not in an hour, not by tomorrow, not by sometime next week but I wanted our Lord to forgive me right NOW!

And then, as we know, the prayer goes on to say,"...as I forgive those who have trespassed against me." Once again, it became very crystal clear to me what I was saying and who I was saying it to.

I was asking the all powerful, almighty, sovereign God to forgive me and I was telling Him that I was going to forgive anybody and everybody who had ever done anything to hurt me - not in an hour, not tomorrow, not even next week - I was telling God I was going to forgive them - right NOW.

As soon as those words came out of my mouth, I could think of at least three or four people who had done something to hurt me and I just flat out was not going to forgive them, ever. I immediately felt like a hypocrite - and I was. That's when I realized I needed to be very careful, extremely careful, what I said to God.

Now, the second reason I bring this topic up is that it reminds me of a very powerful example that I think will help you better understand the importance of forgiveness.

Lessons learned in prison

I was asked to do an all-day retreat at the Louisiana state penitentiary. I'm sure most people have no idea of the significance of that particular prison.

First of all, it is the largest maximum security prison in the United States. A number of years ago there was a book written, and a movie produced, called "Dead Man Walking." That's the penitentiary that book and movie were focused on.

It was an extremely unusual retreat.

I presented the spiritual retreat for 150 inmates in an interfaith chapel.

During the entire eight-hour retreat, there were two guards standing in the back of the chapel ... with machine-guns.

I remember praying before the retreat, saying, "Lord, I hope I don't upset those guys!"

Before the retreat started, while I was chatting with the Catholic chaplain, I asked him, "Out of these 150 inmates, what are some of the crimes they've been committing."

Looking at me, he said, "Glenn, if you can think of any crime, these guys have committed it."

Then he told me, "I want you to know at the beginning, these 150 men will show no emotion at all. They will work very hard at letting you know that absolutely nothing you are saying is penetrating their minds or their hearts, because if they show any emotion at all, it will be looked upon as a sign of weakness by the other inmates and they will be taken advantage of."

So, just as he warned me, those 150 inmates sat in their chairs for the entire eight-hour retreat, with their arms crossed, just trying to stare me down.

Well, early in the program, I had just finished giving a presentation on unforgiveness and forgiveness. We had taken a break and I had walked over to the drinking fountain.

That's when I looked up and realized that this unique, original, masterpiece of God - who must have been every bit of six-foot-five-inches tall, and must have weighed at least 350 pounds, with every inch of his skin that I could see covered with tattoos - was walking toward me.

I thought, "Oh, Lord!"

This guy got right up close, in my face. His nose was literally touching my own nose. And the reason he was getting so close is that he didn't want anybody else to hear what he was about to say to me.

He looked at me and said, "Can you help me with this unforgiveness stuff?"

"Well, I'll try," I told him. "Could you be more specific?"

"Yes, I can," he said. "I need to forgive myself and one other person."

"OK, can you be even more specific?," I asked.

He said, "Yes, I killed the man who killed my wife and daughter."

Now, folks, I'm not generally at a loss for words. But, in an instant, I saw what unforgiveness could do. It took the life, the physical life, of three people who are gone and they are never coming back.

And, this man, who I found out later was 26 years old, was locked away in this prison for the rest of his life - which is not where God originally created this man to spend his life.

You see, unforgiveness is a terminal illness.

Sometimes, unforgiveness can kill us physically. At times, it will kill us spiritually. And, at times, it will kill us emotionally.

In fact, unforgiveness also is ripping our society apart. Marriages and families are broken apart by unforgiveness.

Parents don't talk to their children. Children don't talk to their parents. Aunts don't talk to uncles. Brothers don't talk to sisters.

Unforgiveness is even ripping apart many church communities.

I know this may be hard for you to believe, but when I go into some churches, I see people hold hands during the Lord's prayer, then see those same people walk down the center aisle to receive the body, blood, soul and divinity of Jesus Christ and then they will walk out of the doors of their church after Mass and refuse to talk to one another.

I don't understand that. They have just received Jesus Christ into their lives and their hearts, their soul and their being. Yet they walk out of their church and they see somebody they don't like and look at them like something they don't like on the bottom of their shoe.

Folks, that's not Christian. And, it's not Catholic.

When our hearts become that hard we will do things we shouldn't, we will say things that will embarrass us and we will treat people like we would never treat them if we had a soft heart.

In my studies of scripture, one of the things I became very aware of is that Jesus knew He didn't have very long on this Earth.

Also, Jesus never stayed in one place very long. He went from towns to villages and to cities and sometimes only stayed a few hours, so Jesus had to make sure that when He preached a message there would be no doubt that the people understood what He was telling them.

So, whenever we want to know the truth about a particular topic, it's important that we go to the master teacher, and that's Jesus.

Unforgiveness is one of God's toughest lessons to take to heart

One thing Jesus was very, very clear about was forgiveness and unforgiveness.

Here's the Gospel of Matthew 6:14-15, with these words of Jesus Christ:

"If you forgive others their transgressions, your heavenly Father will forgive you. But, if you do not forgive others, neither will your Father in heaven forgive your transgressions."

Now, my brothers and sisters, a five-year-old child could understand those words of Jesus.

He was saying to all of us that if we forgive people who have offended and hurt us, our heavenly Father will forgive us for offending Him and others.

But, if we decide not to forgive, our heavenly Father will not forgive us.

At my age, the most important thing I want in my life is my heavenly Father's forgiveness.

I will do anything and everything, to the best of my ability, to make sure that I have forgiven everyone in my life for their trespasses against me.

Then I will know that I have a clean slate so that my Lord will forgive me for my transgressions against Him and against the people in my life.

You may think that I've always been a forgiving person, so of course I can't understand other people, especially Christians, when they're not forgiving of those who offend them or hurt them.

That's just not true.

For many, many years - most of my life, actually - even though Jesus tried to make this message about forgiveness very clear to me in the Bible, I had a great misunderstanding and unwillingness about this whole concept of forgiveness and unforgiveness.

I used to think that when somebody hurt me in one way or another, if I forgave that person then what I was also saying to them was that what they did to me was okay.

But, because what they did to me was not okay, I went around practically my whole life holding on to unforgiveness. It seemed perfectly right to me.

However, I've learned that when we forgive someone, we are not telling them that it was okay.

We should forgive others for a few very important reasons. First, because our Lord and Savior Jesus Christ said to do it. Remember that His final words on this earth, during His final agony after mistreatment by others, in his final moments of life on this earth set the right example for all of us.

Even as they were scourging Him and beating him and spitting on him and calling him every bad name in the book, and even while they were nailing him to a wooden cross for an excruciatingly painful death, He looked down at the same people who were killing Him and prayed, "Father, forgive them."

Jesus set the example of forgiveness for all of us. You know, that should have been a clear enough lesson for any of us. Our Lord Jesus told us to forgive, so we should forgive, and that's the end of that.

But, you know, for most of us that's never quite good enough.

Now, another reason we should forgive - and it's really fair to call it a selfish reason - is that when we forgive someone of a wrong, we are also being good to ourselves.

You see, if we are holding any unforgiveness against anybody in our lives, past or present, it's the same as if we had placed ourselves in a prison cell. Nobody else has put us there. We have put ourselves there.

Fortunately, the handle to this prison cell door is on the inside, where we can easily reach it. So, when we forgive we are letting ourselves out of that cell and setting ourselves free, breaking the chains of imprisonment that had bound us.

As you can see, even if we think it's not important for us to forgive someone just because our Lord and Savior has told us we should, it is worthwhile to do it because we want to be good to ourselves.

One of the roadblocks that used to hinder my willingness to forgive was that I used to believe that if I forgave someone, I was required to re-establish a relationship with that person. Yes, many of the people who had hurt me in some way were people whom I had no desire to ever have a relationship with again.

Then I discovered that restoring a relationship is not one of God's requirements for forgiveness. Jesus told us to forgive but we can make our own decision about whether we have a relationship or a friendship with those people we forgive.

Today, there are people that I have forgiven and I made the decision to re-establish a relationship with them because I knew it was what God wanted.

But, there are other people in my life that I have forgiven without making the decision to have a relationship with them because I knew it would not be good for me or for them. Some relationships are just not healthy or safe!

In my life, which I'm sure in most ways is not very different from your own, I have discovered four things that have helped me to learn to forgive. Maybe, at some point, when you're dealing with feelings of unforgiveness against somebody, you will remember these things. I really think they will help you.

The first thing that has helped me to forgive somebody is prayer. Jesus said in Luke 6:28, "Pray for those who mistreat you."

Have you ever prayed for somebody that you just don't like? I know I have and I've got to tell you, at first I was just not very sincere.

"Oh, Lord,. Bless this person, give him some help, watch over him..." - that sort of thing.

But, if I make a conscious, deliberate decision to pray for somebody that I'm having a hard time with, every single day, then at some point in my decision to do that, my anger, my resentment, my unforgiveness is just gone.

I don't know how that happens, but remember, all of this is so spiritual. This is a spiritual, divine principle we're involved with; something that our finite, limited, human brains just can't figure out.

The second thing, after prayer, is humility. We cannot be filled with pride and really, truly forgive someone, or allow them to forgive us. Look at the cross, the crucifix, in any Catholic church or Catholic home. His enemies stripped our Lord, Jesus Christ, of every bit of pride He might have had.

He had no pride left as He died on the cross. Yet He showed us one of the greatest and most humbling acts anyone ever could, forgiving His tormentors as He hung there, dying on that cross.

So far, we have prayer and humility to help us forgive. The third thing we need is to have the willingness to forgive. For forgiveness to be truly effective, we have to want to do it. That's when forgiveness becomes a decision of your will. It's not a decision based on your feelings.

I used to think that when my decision felt good, I would forgive. No, it's the other way around. When I forgive, then my decision will feel good.

Remember that old "forgive and forget" saying?

A lot of people never forgive because they think they have to forget the incident, and they can't forget it. Actually, you will probably never, ever forget what happened.

Don't make that mistake, thinking you have to be able to forget whatever happened before you can forgive a person for it. Don't refuse another person's request for your forgiveness just because you feel you can't ever forget what happened.

I know, because I used to use all kinds of excuses not to be forgiving. But, at some point, forgiveness must become a conscious, willing decision.

You know, in the hundreds of missions and retreats I've given, I've had many, many people come up to me afterward and say, "Glenn, I can't forgive that person, I just can't."

After listening to them for a while, I tell them, "I have to respectfully say to you, forgiveness has nothing to do with 'can't,' it has to do with 'won't!'"

Forgiveness must become a decision of the will. We either choose to forgive somebody or we choose not to forgive them. When we use the excuse 'I can't,' we think that takes us off the hook. After all, if we simply can't forgive someone then that settles that. We're off the hook and we're okay.

My friends, Jesus wants us to be forgiving people and He would never ask us to do anything that He knew we didn't have the ability to do, with His grace.

So, why is this thing about making a decision of your will so important?

Let me give you a very, very powerful example.

A number of years ago I was giving a parish mission and we were staying at the rectory of the church. A parishioner came up to me one day and asked if she could make an appointment to see me.

We made that appointment, she came to the rectory, sat down in one of the offices with me and started sharing her long-time feelings of unforgiveness she had against her mother for something that had happened when she was just a little child.

This woman had been carrying around this unforgiveness for so long that she had become so bitter and angry toward her mother that it had become like a poison, an acid that was eating away at her insides.

As she began to share this emotional, traumatic situation with me, I saw her physical features actually begin to change. That tells you how angry and bitter this woman was.

Well, after about 20 minutes of this, I stopped her and I said, "Now, you already know what Jesus wants you to do."

"Yes, I know," she said.

"And, you know what our Catholic church wants you to do..."

"Yes, I know that, too," she said.

I asked her if her mother was anywhere in the area so she could go and try to reconcile this relationship?

"My mom's been dead for 20 years," she said.

Who was hurting?

Certainly not her mom!

It was as if this beautiful woman got up every morning, fixed breakfast, got dressed and, before she got to the front door of her home to leave, she wrapped herself in about 500 pounds of chains, then opened her door and walked out to start her day.

I'm telling you, it was literally killing her.

I could see it in her face.

Well, the last night of the mission, this woman walked through the door of the church and the moment I saw her walk in I knew something had happened that day. Something had changed in her life.

You see, the first three nights of the mission this beautiful woman had worn very dark clothing, and she never, ever smiled. As far as she was concerned, she had nothing to smile about. Clearly, the unforgiveness she carried around with her had taken all of the joy out of her life.

This time as she walked in, she wore a bright yellow dress and had a smile that lit up that whole church.

I walked up to her, greeted her and asked, "What happened to you?"

"Glenn, I went to my mom's grave for the first time in 20 years. I stood at her grave and asked her to forgive me for everything and anything I had ever done to hurt her.

"And then, Glenn, I forgave my mom for anything and everything she had ever done to hurt me. It feels like 10,000 pounds have been lifted off of my shoulders."

And, then, what she said next convinced me that this beautiful woman, who was having her life restored by God through forgiveness, really "got it," really understood that lesson about forgiveness.

"Glenn," she said, "I don't know, and I may never know, how much joy and hope and peace and love I have lost over the past 20 years because I refused to forgive. I refused to let it go."

105

Remember what I said, unforgiveness is a terminal illness. If we let it stay, it will eventually destroy us and, then, it will eventually kill us, spiritually and physically.

I don't know about you but so much of my understanding about unforgiveness and forgiveness is all tied up in God's sacrament of reconciliation, given to the Catholic church. I have experienced a roller coaster of emotions when it comes to this sacrament. Perhaps you have, too.

Growing up as a little Catholic kid in San Diego, Calif., the church I grew up in was like every other Catholic church way back then. We had confessions every Saturday from 3:30 p.m. to 4:30 p.m.

My mom, God bless her, would encourage me to go to confession every Saturday. I'll never forget this one particular Saturday. I was 10 years old. I wasn't a saint growing up but, all-in-all, I wasn't a bad kid. I was a good kid, by all measures.

One Saturday morning, about 10 a.m., I went to my mom and told her, "Mom, guess what?! I had an absolutely terrific week. I didn't sin. So I don't have to go to confession."

Well, she looked at me and said, "Oh, yes, you do! Now, you go back into your room and you figure out what you've done."

So, I went back to my room and I must have spent an hour trying to figure out what I had done. Then I went to her again and said, "Mom, I can't think of anything." She said, "By the time you get to church, you will."

My Dad drove me to church, about a 20-minute drive, and I was literally sweating bullets because I couldn't think of anything to confess. So I walked into the church and, fortunately for me, there were 20 people standing in line. You don't see that anymore. Well, the line kept getting shorter and shorter and shorter and I still couldn't even begin to think of anything.

I was standing right by the door and a school friend came up. I asked him, "Who's hearing confessions?"

When he told me, I said, "Ohhh, no!"

Then I went into the confessional, the door closed behind me and it was real dark in there. For those readers who are my age, you know what that means. So I knelt down and suddenly that little window opened up.

What I heard sounded just like the voice of God coming from the other side of that screen.

"Yes, my child!" the priest said.

I froze. I still couldn't think of anything.

Then came that voice again: "Yes, my child!"

"Bless me Father for I have sinned. It has been a week since my last confession," I said, knowing the usual starting point. From there, I blundered on.

"These are my sins," I said. "I stole my brother's baseball glove and when my brother found out we got into this terrible fight and I'm sorry."

There was a pause and then the priest said, "Now, son, you know you're not supposed to take things that don't belong to you."

I said, "Yes, Father."

"And, you're certainly not supposed to fight with your brother," he said.

I said, "Yes, Father."

Then he gave me my penance and as I was walking out of the confessional I thought to myself, "If he just knew that I was an only child!"

Then it dawned on me, I had just lied to a priest. I avoided him like the plague for at least three weeks, because I just knew if he heard my voice he was going to want to meet my brother.

Isn't it amazing what we do to ourselves.

Growing up as a little Catholic kid, I saw this sacrament simply and only as a laundry list of sins. I went in week after week after week saying the same thing over and over and over again.

I know none of you reading this book ever did that. It was just me - right?!

Then, I moved into my teenage years and something miraculous happened when I went from 12 to 13. When I became a teenager I literally gained divine wisdom overnight. At the exact same time, my parents lost all of their intelligence. As a teenager, nothing my parents could say to me made any sense. They were old fashioned, they were irrelevant, they were out of touch, they didn't "get it."

You know, I viewed my Catholic church in the same way.

My Catholic church was out of touch and old fashioned.

It was boring and it was out of step - especially when it came to the Sacrament of Reconciliation. I began to rationalize my sins. I got so good at rationalizing my sins that I even reached the point where I rationalized that I didn't sin. If I didn't sin, then why would I need to go to Reconciliation?

As a result, I went to reconciliation one time during all of my teenage years, and that was right before my confirmation.

Many years ago, someone interviewed Pope Pius XII. They asked him what he thought was the greatest sin of the 20th Century in our world.

He said, "The greatest sin of the 20th Century is that we have lost our sense of sin."

Nothing is a sin anymore.

It's simply - a mistake.

Well, if it's just a mistake, then why do I need to go ask forgiveness for a mistake?

But, later on, when I moved into my young adult years, my wife Linda and I got married and we had our first daughter, Christina. When she was about seven years old, she was preparing at our church for her first Sacrament of Reconciliation.

Of course, she had brought a book home from her religious education class and she came up to me one Saturday morning and said, "Daddy, will you help me prepare? Would you help me go through this book?"

"Oh, sure," I said.

So we sat on the couch and we were going through this book for about 15 or 20 minutes when she suddenly stopped, looked up at me, and said, "Dad, is this important, what I'm doing?"

"Yes," I told her, "It's very important."

She said, "OK," and we continued working our way through this religious Catholic lesson book.

About 30 minutes later, she stopped me again, and asked, "Dad, are you sure that this Sacrament of Reconciliation, and what I am preparing to do, is important?"

"Christina," I said, looking directly into her eyes, "It is one of the most important things you will ever do in your life."

Then, came the message. She said, "Dad, if it's that important for me, why isn't it that important for you?"

You see, she could see that I was telling her with my mouth that it was important for her to go to the Sacrament of Reconciliation, but she could clearly see from my actions that it really wasn't important at all for me. Looking back, it still just breaks my heart to think of that moment.

But today, as I cross back and forth across this country presenting our missions, I see parents and grandparents constantly telling their children and grandchildren, "Go to confession. Go to confession. It's important that you go."

Sadly, those children and grandchildren never see parents or their grandparents going to confession. What are we really telling those children!?

What hypocritical message are we sending to our children?

Then, as I moved into my middle-adult years, and there was a time in our married life when Linda and I had problems, became separated and almost got a divorce, but then we renewed our wedding vows.

Well, about four months after we had renewed our wedding vows, I remember I was at church for some reason or another on a Saturday afternoon and I was walking across the parking lot of the church.

That was just at the moment when our pastor, who had an absolutely incredible gift of wisdom, saw me there and he yelled out to me, called me over and we visited for a while.

Then, he asked me a question, "Glenn, how's your marriage?" "Oh, Father, it's never been better, it's never been stronger," I told him.

"Have you forgiven Linda for anything that she might have said or done to hurt you during those tough times?," he asked.

I said, "Absolutely!"

He said, "Have you forgiven your two daughters for anything that they might have said, or for any ways that they might have treated you during that time?"

I said, "You bet I have."

"Now I know that our faith community said some very mean things about you during that time. Have you forgiven them?" he asked. I said, "Yes, Father, I have."

Then he looked at me and asked, "Glenn, have you forgiven yourself?"

Well, he caught me with that one.

I thought I had done something that was unforgivable and if I couldn't forgive myself, how could God possibly forgive me?

When Father saw my hesitation, he grabbed my arm and started walking me to the church. And, I surely knew where he was taking me. So I stopped him right in the middle of that parking lot and I said, "Father, I know where you're taking me and I can't go."

You see, despite all that I'd been through, I hadn't gone to confession in probably fifteen years.

I knew the words had changed, I told him, and I knew the formulas have changed, but he stopped me right there, looked me in the eye and said, "Jesus is not so concerned that you get all the words just right, that's what I'm here to help you with. What Jesus and I want to know right now is do you truly want to be reconciled with God and with yourself?"

"More than anything in my life," I told him.

"Come with me," he said.

I want to tell you, my brothers and sisters, when I left that Sacrament and walked out of the doors of that church, that was the first time in my life that I truly understood, in the depths of my mind, my heart and my spirit, what Jesus and my Catholic church had been trying to tell me all those years.

I had a peace, a hope, a joy and a feeling of love that just goes beyond all understanding. I felt like I could have literally floated across that parking lot.

Now, honestly, I would never think of asking you to do something that I wasn't willing to do myself.

But now that I've come to grips with the Sacrament of Reconciliation, and have found so much peace and happiness from it, I certainly do recommend that all of you readers do the same.

110

Please, go to confession, with an open mind and heart. See this great Sacrament of our Catholic church in a new light, a Sacrament not of punishment but of freeing forgiveness offered by our God and Savior, Jesus Christ.

He knows our human nature and our needs, how we make mistakes and how much we need to ask his forgiveness and others' forgiveness, including forgiving ourselves.

Now, here's another example, one that may remind you of similar challenging moments in your own life.

I want to take you back to December of 1995, when our youngest daughter, Kelly, started dating this man.

You know, I don't know how to say this except just to say it. I didn't like her boyfriend. And, I let him know it every way that I could.

We were living in Louisiana then and our kids were on the West Coast, so about that time we flew out to California for Christmas. On Christmas Eve, we were at our oldest daughter's house, with her husband, Dan, and our first granddaughter, Danielle.

I heard that Kelly was coming over. I also heard that Zane, the boyfriend I didn't like, wasn't coming. Believe me, I was happy about that. I had an absolutely wonderful Christmas.

So we came back home, another year went by and, once again, for Christmas 1996, Linda and I flew back out to California. It was Christmas Eve and again we were at our oldest daughter's house.

Now between Christmas 1995 and Christmas 1996, Kelly and Zane were married welcomed their first child, our second granddaughter, Zoe. I heard that Kelly was coming for Christmas again this year, of course, and bringing Zoe. But, this time, I heard that my new son-in-law was coming, too. And, I had no idea what I was going to do.

About 9 p.m. on Christmas Eve, Kelly and Zane and Zoe hadn't arrived yet. That's when Linda walked up to me and asked, "Glenn, what are you going to do?"

"I don't know," I said.

Then, Christina walked up to me.

"Dad, what are you going to do?"

"I don't know," I said.

By then, I even expected their cat to come over and ask me what I was going to do when Zane arrived with his wife, Kelly, and their first child.

Here I was, this Catholic evangelist who was running all over this country telling everybody else they're supposed to forgive and my own family could see, up close and personal, that I wasn't doing it.

Suddenly, there was a knock on the door. Christina opened the door and there was Kelly, holding Zoe.

I was sitting in a chair and Kelly came over and gave me a big hug and put Zoe in my arms. It was the first time I'd seen my second granddaughter and I'm loving her and kissing her.

But, that's when I noticed out of the corner of my eye that Zane was at the front door. He still hadn't come in.

Well, I handed Zoe back to Kelly and got up, walked over to Zane, put my arms around him. His body was as hard as a piece of wood.

I remember saying, under my breath, "Oh, Lord, don't fail me now."

Suddenly, I felt Zane's arms come up as he reached around me and squeezed me so tight I thought I was going to break.

Then, he began to shake, and I realized he was crying. Then, I started to cry. Out of the corner of my eye, I could see my whole family standing nearby - and they were crying. That's when I caught sight of my daughter, Kelly, this beautiful child of God, and I realized what I had done to her by rejecting Zane.

The two most important men in her life - her husband and her father - had not talked to each other in more than a year. And, I was the one to blame, the one who had caused that.

That's when I had to make a decision of the will.

I knew that this unforgiveness was killing me. It was killing my family, it was killing my daughter and I had to make a decision of the will to either continue to hold onto this attitude of mine - which meant destroying myself and everyone around me who loved me - or I was going to make a decision of the will to be forgiving.

Remember, forgiveness - no matter how difficult or stressful - is something we can do with God's help.

So, at that moment, I made a decision of my will to forgive Zane and to ask him to forgive me. We were all set free!

Now, I'd like to do something that, for our readers, may very well be one of the holiest parts of this entire chapter on making "decisions of the will," those decisions where we don't know how we're going to do it, but we know that we must do it because it's what God clearly wants us to do.

Think about this part of the chapter as an examination of your conscience, in which you will have an opportunity - if you choose - to forgive whatever you have against anyone. I invite you to get as comfortable as you can, wherever you are reading this, and as I mention various people it will be helpful for you to visualize each person in the presence of our Lord.

Ask God to give you the grace, as you read this, to forgive where forgiveness is needed.

Lord, Jesus, I ask you for the grace to forgive everyone in my life. I thank you, Lord, that you love me more than I love myself, and that you want my happiness even more than I desire it myself.

So, Lord, I choose to forgive myself, for my sins, my faults and my failings. I forgive myself for anything I have done to hurt you or to hurt anyone else. Today, I forgive myself.

Lord Jesus, please forgive me for the times I have been angry, bitter or resentful toward you. When I blamed you, Lord, for the hard times, the financial difficulties or the death that came into my family.

Please, forgive me, Lord.

Lord, I choose now to forgive my mother and my father for all the times they may have hurt me. I forgive them for any lack of support, love, affection or attention. And, Lord, please forgive me for the times that I hurt or sinned against my mother and my father, in any way.

Lord Jesus, I forgive my spouse, or my ex-spouse, for any love, affection, consideration, support or attention they have not shown to me and I forgive them for their faults, weaknesses, hurtful words or actions.

And, please forgive me, Lord, for any time or in any way, that I have hurt my spouse, sinned against her or withheld any of my love, attention, affection or support.

Lord Jesus, I choose now to forgive my brothers and my sisters for the times that they may have hurt me, resented me or competed for my parents' love and affection. I forgive them for the times that they may have physically or emotionally harmed me. And, please forgive me, Lord, for the times that I have hurt or in any way sinned against my brothers or my sisters.

Lord, Jesus, I forgive my children and grandchildren for any lack of respect, obedience, love, attention, warmth and understanding. And, Lord, please forgive me for any time I ever hurt or sinned against my children or grandchildren.

Lord, I forgive all of my relatives who have interfered in our family and brought dissension. I forgive them for any times at which they have hurt my wife, my children or me. And please forgive me, Lord, for any times that I have hurt or sinned against any of my relatives.

Lord, Jesus, I forgive my co-workers, my employer or former employer or employees for the times that they may have gossiped about me or would not cooperate. I forgive them for the times they were disagreeable or made my life miserable in any way. And, please forgive me, Lord, for the times that I was guilty of those same sins.

Lord, I choose now to also forgive any bishops, priests, deacons, sisters, religious or any members of my church community for any way in which they may have hurt me.

Lord, I forgive them for all of their weaknesses, faults and their failings. And, Lord, please forgive me for any time or in any way that I have hurt any bishops, priests, deacons, sisters, religious or any members of my church community.

Lord Jesus, I forgive any professional people for any way that they may have hurt me. I forgive doctors, nurses, lawyers, police, teachers, social workers, principals or politicians for any way, at any time, that they may have hurt me. Please forgive me for any way or any time that I have hurt or sinned against any of them.

Lord Jesus, please forgive me for not seeing others as my brothers and sisters and as temples of your Holy Spirit.

Lord, please forgive me for my prejudices, my biases, my using and abusing others, and, Lord, please forgive others who have been guilty of these same sins.

Finally, Lord, I ask for the grace to forgive that one person who has hurt me the most, that one person that I consider my greatest enemy, that one person, Lord, I find hardest to forgive, in fact, Lord, that one person that I said I would never forgive.

Lord, please, free me of the burden of unforgiveness and fill my life with your peace.

Lord Jesus, you know our needs. We want to be free of all of our burdens, Lord. Please drive out the darkness of unforgiveness and fill our hearts with your light.

Lord, help me to forgive all of these people, including myself, and to accept your forgiveness, right now.

My brothers and sisters, I pray - as you're reading these pages - that these prayers will leave you liberated, set free of any anger, any resentment, any bitterness, any unforgiveness in your life.

I ask our God's forgiveness for each and every one of us, in Jesus' name. Amen.

Our Closing Prayer

Lord, we thank you for being present to those who are reading these pages. I ask that you surround all those who read this book with your holy ministering and protecting angels. Lord, heal them in every area of their life that has been in need of healing and renewal and restoration. Lord, grant them every desire, every prayer and every petition of their hearts, according to your will.

And, Lord, give them patience to wait for your answer, faith to accept whatever your answer is and courage to continue to live your gospel. We ask all of these things in the precious and holy name of our Lord and our Savior, Jesus Christ.

Amen.

A Call to Action

1. Prior to reading this chapter, what was your understanding of forgiveness?

2. Currently, who are the person(s) in your life whom you are struggling with forgiving?

3. What roadblocks are holding you back from forgiving them?

4. What specific actions can you take to remove those roadblocks?

5. If you're Catholic, what is your current understanding of our Church's Sacrament of Reconciliation?

6. As you read or prayed through the forgiveness prayers, did you forgive   anyone?
   If so, who?

7. Is there anyone you are unwilling to forgive at this point? If so, go back to question #3.

Chapter 5

When The Rubber
Meets The Road

Now that you have made the commitment to read this book to strengthen your relationship with God and your church, keep an open mind and an open heart, willing to receive whatever God has in store for you. He will bless you beyond your wildest dreams.

Now most of us are aware that the road to Emmaus is a very powerful Scripture, found in the Gospel of Luke. As we conclude these chapters, it is very appropriate that we look at that particular Gospel, in the 24th Chapter beginning with verse 13.

To start out, let me remind you that this particular Scripture takes place shortly after our Lord's crucifixion. It centers on two disciples who had put all of their trust, all of their hope, all of their faith in this man called Jesus.

They had made the decision to believe that Jesus was really who He said He was, that He was the Messiah, the Jesus, the Christ, the Savior of the world.

Then, they watched Jesus Christ being nailed to a cross and die.

As they walked away from Calvary, as they left Jerusalem to walk to a town called Emmaus, you can imagine what these two disciples were going through.

If you had put all of your trust, hope and faith in someone who then appeared to have let you down, you can just imagine that the disciples were sad, they were angry, depressed, confused and they had lots of doubts and questions.

That's where this Scripture begins, in the Gospel of Luke, 24:13.

"Now that very day two of them were going to a village, seven miles from Jerusalem, called Emmaus. And, they were conversing about all the things that had occurred and it happened that while they were conversing and debating, Jesus Himself drew near. But their eyes were prevented from recognizing him."

Let's stop here for just a minute.

There are all kinds of theology and all kinds of theories about why these two disciples who knew Jesus intimately did not recognize the risen Christ. I believe one of the reasons is they did not expect to see Him. Everything about them was still stuck at Calvary. In their minds, in their hearts and as far as they were concerned, Jesus Christ was dead.

So often, in our own lives - in fact, I believe that every day of our lives - the risen Jesus stands right in front of us yet so often we don't see Him, we don't recognize Him, because in at least one area of our lives we are still stuck at Calvary. Until we let go of those Calvary experiences we will never truly recognize the living Christ in our lives.

Well, Jesus goes on to say, "What are you discussing as you walk along?"

They stopped, looking downcast, and one of them, Cleopas, said to Him in reply, "Are you the only visitor to Jerusalem who does not know the things that have taken place there in these days?"

Jesus replied to them, "What kinds of things?"

Now I find this very fascinating. Jesus is the Lord. Jesus knows everything. He knew exactly what these two disciples were talking about. He knew the thoughts in their minds. He knew the pain and the questions in their hearts.

He could have, if He wanted to, told them everything that they were thinking about, but all Jesus said was, "What kinds of things?"

You see, the Lord knew that for their healing to take place these two disciples had to get it out, they had to share whatever was going on in their minds and hearts. Just like in our lives, Jesus looks at you and me and says, "What kinds of things?"

Jesus so much wants us to talk with Him. He wants us to share with Him all of the joys and blessings of our lives.

But, He also wants us to share with Him all of our doubts, concerns and fears. That's exactly what He was asking these two disciples.

"The things that happened to Jesus, the Nazarean," they replied. "He was a prophet, mighty in deed and word before God and all the people. Our chief priests and rulers handed Him over to a sentence of death and crucified Him. We were hoping He would be the one to redeem Israel.

"Besides all this, it is now the third day since this has taken place. Some women from our group, however, have astounded us. They were in the tomb early in the morning and they did not find His body. They came back and reported that they had indeed seen a vision of angels who announced that He was alive. Then some of those with us went to the tomb and found things just as the women had described, but Him they did not see."

Then Jesus said to them, "Oh, how foolish you are. How slow of heart to believe all that the prophets spoke. Was it not necessary that the Messiah should suffer these things before He entered into His glory?"

Then, beginning with Moses and all of the prophets, He interpreted to them what referred to Himself in all of the Scriptures.

As they approached the village to where they were going He gave the impression that He was going on farther but they urged Him, "Stay with us, for it is nearly evening and the day is almost over."

Now let's stop here again. I find this extremely fascinating. Just a few miles down the road, Jesus approached these two disciples and as far as they're concerned, He's a stranger. But after a few miles of walking down this road together, sharing with Jesus everything in their minds and hearts and then listening to Jesus explain to them everything about Himself, a relationship began to develop.

When Jesus was about ready to leave, there was such a bond that had been established in just a few miles, that they said, "Oh, please don't go!"

Every day of your life, do you say, "Oh, Jesus, please don't go?" Do you have such a relationship with our Lord, Jesus Christ, that you just say, "Oh, Lord, please don't go?"

"So Jesus went in to stay with them," Scripture says, "and it happened that while He was with them at table, He took bread, said the blessing, broke it and gave it to them. With that their eyes were opened and as they recognized Him He vanished from their sight."

Then they said to each other, "Were not our hearts burning within us while He spoke to us on the way and opened the Scriptures to us?"

So they set out at once and returned to Jerusalem where they found gathered together the 11 apostles and those with them who were saying, "The Lord has truly been raised and has appeared to Simon."

Then the two recounted what had taken place on their journey and how Jesus "was made known to them in the breaking of the bread." At this very moment, this is where this Scripture coincides and intersects with the final chapter of this book. In that gospel, after those two disciples had recognized Jesus Christ as He vanished from their sight, they turned around and went back to Jerusalem.

They went back to their homes and their families and friends, to a lot of people who still did not believe and were doubting that Jesus had truly risen from the dead.

They then had an opportunity to share their relationship with Jesus Christ.

At the end of this book, you will have the same opportunity as those two disciples did 2,000 years ago. When you are with your family, your neighbors, those you work with at your job, those you see at your church, you will have that same opportunity to share your relationship with Jesus Christ.

I am a firm believer that if a person like you makes the decision to read a book like this but, at the end, closes the cover and nothing has changed, if you don't have a deeper, stronger relationship with our Lord, if you don't have a closer bond to one another, then you've missed the whole point of this book.

You see, this is where the rubber meets the road. This final chapter is all about commitment - or, for many of you, a re-commitment - to Jesus Christ.

If we're going to do what Jesus asks us to do, we must believe that Jesus is who He says He is, and we must understand the commitment that Christ made to us.

A number of years ago, after one of our missions, a lady came up to me and asked a question that at first astounded me. She said, "Why should I make a deeper commitment to Jesus Christ. What did Jesus Christ ever do for me?"

When she asked me that question, I was speechless for a while. I couldn't believe that this woman honestly did not realize what Jesus had done for her. Perhaps, as you are finishing this last chapter, you may have that same question.

Quite often, as we travel this country giving these spiritual missions, someone will come up to me and say, "Isn't our cross beautiful?"

In a very loving way, not intending to hurt anyone, I will look at them and say, "That's the problem. That cross is beautiful."

If you had been at the foot of the cross at Calvary 2,000 years ago, I can guarantee you, that cross was not beautiful! It was bloody, it was ugly, it was painful. I don't think it's on purpose but I think over the past 2,000 years of salvation history we have cleaned up, watered down and sterilized that commitment that Christ made to us 2,000 years ago.

That's why, in this last chapter of our book, we're going to take a very hard and serious look at the commitment that Jesus made for us.

Many years ago, I came across a powerful depiction of the crucifixion. Now, I want you to know, I've read the story of His crucifixion about 200 times but it is still difficult for me to read. And, it might be difficult for some of you to read.

But, just imagine, if it is difficult for you to read this now, how difficult and painful it must have been for Jesus to go through this.

At this time, I'd like you to - as best you can, in your mind's eye - take yourself back 2,000 years and place yourself at the foot of the cross. Try to get in touch with what it must have sounded like at Calvary, even what it might have looked like, what it smelled like.

Are you ready? Have you mentally taken yourself back 2,000 years?

Scourging and crucifixion were so common that the gospel writers do not give us much understanding of it. For example, in a three-day period, 10,000 men were crucified on a stretch of road 19 miles long. When we say Jesus died for us, we have little understanding of the mental and spiritual suffering He endured for us. That is beyond our ability to understand.

The physical aspect, however, we can examine to gain a better understanding of His sacrifice

Crucifixion is torture. Invented by the Persians, crucifixion means the attachment of a person to a cross by nails driven through hands and feet. The Romans developed an extremely high degree of efficiency and skill with crucifixion.

They were such experts that they could even determine how quickly a man would die, often predicting within an hour of when a man would die.

Earlier in Roman history, when they crucified men in trees, they would live from five to 15 days. Jesus, however, was so exhausted that He was practically dead by the time they nailed Him to the cross, which is why He died so quickly .

There are all kinds of opinions of what a cross weighed, but estimates range from 100 to 200 pounds. This is the burden Jesus was attempting to carry on his back from the fortress in Antonia to Golgotha.

The passion of Jesus begins in the garden of Gethsemane. Scripture tells us that Jesus prayed so long that His sweat became drops of blood trickling down upon the ground. Jesus was going through such agony! At this point, His agony is so intense that He is almost in shock.

Then, Jesus is arrested.

This is when the physical torture is inflicted. The soldiers begin to strike Him across His face to make Him remain silent as He is questioned. The guards blindfold Him and taunt Him. They call Him names and make great sport of Him. They spit on Him, they strike Him on the face and still there is no protest from Jesus.

By early morning, Jesus is battered and bruised, dehydrated, exhausted and almost unrecognizable. He is tired. He has lost blood. He is emotionally drained. He has no water, no food, no bath, no rest and no refreshments. And those whom He had chosen to continue His ministry have deserted Him.

His enemies had planned for months how they would get rid of Jesus. So they took him to Pilate. Pilate didn't want to kill Jesus but he did have Him scourged. You see when they scourge a man and then crucify him, that's like double jeopardy, equivalent to sending a man to prison for 30 years and then executing him.

Scourging meant that they stripped Jesus of His robe, and tied Him to a post that was four or five feet high. He could neither stand straight nor fall to the ground. A Roman soldier would walk toward Him with a whip, which was about four to six feet long, with several leather thongs on it. Two or three small balls of lead or bone were attached to the ends of those thongs.

The whip is brought down with full force, again and again, across the shoulders, the back and the legs of Jesus. The cuts go through His skin. As the blows continue they cut deeper into His tissue, producing the oozing of bright red blood from His capillaries, veins and underlying muscles.

The small balls of lead and bone produce large bruises, which become open sores with subsequent blows. The balls are wrapping around His chest, stinging Him like a swarm of bees.

It usually took one-and-a-half to two minutes to beat a man into unconsciousness. The soldiers would not stop beating a man until he was unconscious. Finally, the skin on the back of Jesus is hanging in long ribbons and the entire area is an unrecognizable mass of sores and bleeding tissue.

The Centurion in charge would determine when the prisoner was near death. If he could find a pulse or detect breathing, the beating would continue until the man was no longer breathing or had no detectable pulse.

In other words, they beat Jesus just as close to death as a man could be beaten and still live. Then, and only then, was the scourging stopped. Jesus is untied and allowed to slump to the stone pavement, landing in His own blood.

During this time, the soldiers gathered around and took the opportunity to make great sport of Him. They put a robe on Him and put a stick in His hand as a scepter and they cried out that a king must have a crown, so they take some flexible branches from a tree with long thorns and weave it into a crown, place it on His head and press it into His scalp. Again, there is bleeding.

Then the soldiers take a stick and strike Jesus across the face and head, driving the crown of thorns deeper into His scalp. Finally tired of this sadistic sport, they decided to yank off the robe given to Jesus as they mocked Him as their "king."

By now the robe had stuck to His torn and bloody back. The removal of the robe is equivalent to the careless removal of a surgical bandage, causing excruciating pain. It's almost as though Jesus is being whipped again.

Then, Jesus is turned over to Pilate, who soon gives in to the demands of the crowd that wants Jesus crucified. He gave permission to crucify our Lord, Jesus Christ.

The execution detail of Roman soldiers, headed by a Centurion, began its slow journey. The distance of the walk was about 650 yards. The rough wood was being pressed into His lacerated skin and the muscles of His shoulders. His human muscles are pushed to their endurance limits.

In the Bible, the apostle John reported that there was a company of women following Christ as He carried His cross, including Mary His mother, and Mary Magdalen. This is probably the time when Jesus said, "Weep not for me, but for yourselves."

You see, His suffer ing would soon be over. This is God's own Son, obedient even to death on the cross.

When He reaches Golgatha, Christ is offered some wine drugged to kill the pain, as was the custom. But, Jesus refuses it. Jesus had his feet quickly kicked from under Him and was thrown to the ground. Then, His shoulders are put against the rough wood and a Roman Legionaire feels for the depression at the point of Christ's wrist and drives in the first nail.

Then, he quickly reaches to the other side of Jesus and drives in the other nail, being careful not to get the arms too straight, which leaves Him flexible enough so that Jesus can heave up and down on the cross.

Perhaps you think that the cross was high.

But, you see, Jesus was probably nailed just high enough to get his feet off the ground. You could walk up and look at Jesus right in the eye. Then they'd take the crosspiece, raise it up and put it in a notch on the vertical cross, then quickly nailed His feet.

Then there's the matter of lifting up and down on the cross. They nailed His arms so His body would sag, then they nailed His feet so He could raise up and down to get air.

Soon, the pain would start in other areas. A man who was allowed to sag would soon drown in his own fluids. The pectoral muscles of the chest which expel air would become paralyzed. The air would come in and the pressure would make the lungs feel like they were going to explode. This is when Jesus would raise up one more time to expel that air and take in some fresh oxygen.

When we go to church around Easter time, there's the reading of the beautiful last words of Jesus by someone standing there, well groomed.

But, when they tell us what Jesus has to say, it's a far cry from what took place that day. Sometimes it's made to sound like Jesus simply proclaimed the last words He spoke, when in fact Jesus had to raise himself up with all the strength that was left in Him, just to get those words out.

It was painful. He was dehydrated. His blood became thicker, it becomes hard to pump. Pressure comes on the heart. Pressure comes on the lungs. With every move Jesus makes, His nerves send signals of pain and trauma to His head. Finally, the fluids begin to collect around His heart. As the fluids begin to squeeze in on His heart, everything about Jesus begins to die.

As Scripture says, Jesus was scourged and crucified and then our Lord Jesus died.

My brothers and sisters, this is the ultimate in suffering. Yet this is what the Lord Jesus Christ, our God and our Savior, did for us.

So as you read the Word and it says Jesus was scourged and Jesus was crucified, Jesus died and was resurrected, please keep in mind what He really did for you and me and how blessed we are.

What DID Jesus Christ ever do for you and for me?

As we begin to truly internalize that commitment, that suffering, that ultimate sacrifice, there's absolutely nothing that I wouldn't do for Jesus. I would go anywhere He asked me to go, I would do anything He would ask me to do, I would give up and surrender anything He asked me to give up and surrender because of His commitment to me.

Well, now that we've had that opportunity to look at that commitment that Jesus made for you and for me, what is He asking of us?

My brothers and sisters, Linda and I have been trying to share this with you in the pages of this book.

Jesus doesn't want 50 percent of our minds and hearts and lives. Jesus doesn't want 90 percent. Jesus wants 100 percent of our minds and our hearts and our lives.

He wants us to be willing to remove all of those roadblocks that block our relationship with Him. He wants us to love others as He has loved us and He wants us to forgive others the way He has forgiven us.

That's the commitment that Jesus wants us to make to Him.

But if we are going to make that kind of commitment, there is one thing that we must have an abundance of and that is faith.

So often, I think that we are confused about what faith is, and we make it more complicated than it has to be.

You see, there is a divine part of faith and there is a human part of faith.

I'm going to give you a suggestion. Stop trying to figure out the divine part of faith. Our human, finite brain will never be able to figure out the infinite divine, almighty sovereign God. First of all, to understand faith remember that it is a free gift. We simply have to ask God to give us the gift of faith and continue to ask God to manifest and increase that gift of faith within us.

And, because faith is a free gift we can't buy it. There's not enough money in the world to buy it. We can't earn it, we can't work hard enough to get it. It is a free gift. But our responsibility in this whole thing of faith is to practice our faith.

The Bible is a book of faith. One of the greatest examples of faith was the Apostle Paul. He was beaten, thrown in prison, run out of many towns and villages but he kept preaching about Jesus no matter what the cost to him. He said in Hebrews 11:6, "It is impossible to please God without faith."

I had reached a point in my life many years ago that I truly wanted to please my Lord. Paul was telling me that without faith I couldn't do it. After reading that passage, I never wondered again about the importance of faith.

He also gave us a definition of faith in Hebrews 11:1. He said that "faith is the realization of what is hoped for and the evidence of things not seen."

In other words, when we step out in faith in some area of our lives, we are to realize that what we are hoping for has already happened when at the moment there is no evidence that it has or ever will happen.

That will seem crazy and illogical to the world, as well as to our finite brain. What are you hoping for right now in your life, or in the life of someone else?

The reason you are still hoping is that you haven't seen what you believe is an answer or a resolution. I believe if what you are hoping for is truly in line with the will of God, it is going to happen.

But until it does, you must use St. Paul's definition of faith and put it into practice every day.

You see, faith is leaving the realm of the senses. We live in a society that says if you can't see it, hear it, taste it, touch it or smell it, it doesn't exist.

That's why Jesus said, "Blessed are those who will believe but cannot see."

Jesus knew how hard it would be for us 2,000 years later to believe in Him and His teachings.

I want to share with you a little bit about this whole thing of practicing faith.

We live in a society that says "prove it to us, reveal it to us, show it to us and then we'll believe."

That's the exact opposite of what Jesus Christ tells us.

Jesus says, "Believe first and then as you believe I will show it to you, prove it to you and reveal it to you."

So, faith is all about practice. Once again, let me remind you - I would never ask anybody to do anything that Linda and I have not done ourselves.

First, let me give you a very practical example about faith. Because, as I've said before and say again, we don't want to make this whole faith thing too complicated.

When you leave your home to go to an evening church service, for instance, you probably leave a light on in your home so you don't come home to a dark house.

When you went over and grabbed hold of that light switch, did you look at it and say to yourself, "Now I wonder if I turn this light switch up if the light's going to go on?"

You didn't do that at all, did you? You just walked by, flipped the switch and the light came on. Why? Practice. You have probably, tens of thousands of times in your life, turned the light switch on and off, and you just believe, with everything in you, that when you flip that switch the light's going to go on.

In fact, if you ever flip that switch and the light doesn't go on it shocks you doesn't it? If there's somebody in the house with you, you grab them and say, "Look, the light didn't go on!" You are absolutely astounded that it didn't work.

Are we not supposed to have at least the same amount of faith in the promises of Jesus as we do in the electrical system of our home? You see, I believe that faith has everything to do with believing and hoping and very little about knowing.

Back in July 1992, Linda and I did something that God had been asking us to do for many months.

I want to share with you probably one of the greatest journeys of faith that Linda and I have ever been on.

For months, God had been calling me to give up a very, very successful corporate career. I was vice president of the second largest military distribution company of its kind in the United States. And I had worked very hard to get to that position. Yet I kept hearing God, in various ways, saying, "Glenn, I want you to give all of that up."

You know, sometimes you just kind of pretend you can't hear God?

Sorry, God, wrong frequency! I just can't seem to pick you up!

Well, after a whole series of events, on July 9, 1992, after several months of prodding and poking by God, I walked away from a 20-year corporate career to begin serving our Lord and our Catholic church full time.

And, the very next day, on July 10th, I was so excited. You see, when we begin operating in faith in some area of our lives, we get all caught up in the euphoria of faith.

"OK, Lord, I'm going to go do this!"

The problem is that we often don't stick with our "faith" projects long enough.

And, if we do not burn our bridges behind us, in whatever area where we're moving forward in faith, when it gets tough we will run right back to where it's comfortable.

Well, the very next day I started calling Catholic priests on the phone. I said, "Father, I'm a Catholic evangelist and God has called me to preach and sing. Can I come into your church and do that?"

"No."

I was shocked. I must have contacted 30 or 40 priests and all of them said, "No."

And I didn't understand it. I knew God had called me to do this. I knew God had equipped me to do this. What I couldn't understand is why people weren't calling ME!

Well, Linda and I knew when we started to do this ministry full-time we were going to have to simplify our lives. We had two houses, so we sold both houses and moved into this little, tiny apartment. We could barely walk 10 feet in any direction without hitting a wall. Because of that, we gave away most of our belongings because we couldn't get them into that space.

Also, we began to live off of our savings because we believed it wouldn't be very long before God opened the floodgates of opportunities to preach and sing. Well, a year-and-a-half went by and nobody in the Catholic church wanted to hear us.

However, during that time, I did preach and sing in other churches than Catholic. But God had made it very clear to me that I was a Catholic Christian.

And, this ministry was to be a Catholic Christian ministry for Catholic Christian people.

Well, as I said, 18 months went by and no one of the Catholic faith wanted to hear us.

I had turned over every possible rock looking for opportunities and I was at a loss what to do next. At that point we had only three weeks of money left and then we were going to be broke.

Do you not think that our faith was being tested?

You see, the testing came because I knew that at any time in that year and a half I could pick up the phone and I could have a choice of various corporate jobs.

In fact, many of our friends kept telling us, "Glenn, you can't do this in the Catholic church." And I said, "Why not? God has called us to do this! And, I believe God is going to honor our faith."

Well, one day we got a phone call from a retreat center in Florida and the person on the other end of the phone said, "We understand you are a Christian singer. A Catholic Christian singer."

Absolutely! I told them.

And, I started getting really excited.

The voice on the line said, "Well, we're having a week-long Evangelization retreat and we'd like you to come and do music during the week."

"Wonderful," I said. Now, you've got to know where my mind was. We had only three weeks worth of money left and the first question out of my mouth was, "How much are you going to pay me?"

"Nothing," he said.

Well, I asked him, "You are going to cover our expenses, there and back, aren't you?"

"No," he said. "If you want to come, you just have to come."

I thought, "Well, that's definitely a Catholic retreat center alright."

So I told him I'd get back to him. Then, I went to Linda.

"You know, Honey, this is the first person in a year and a half who's wanted to hear us but if we go it's going to take every bit of money we have left," I said.

Well, we both prayed over that invitation ... and decided to go.

When we got there, they told us they wanted me to sing two songs in the morning and two songs in the afternoon. Well, I did it on Monday and I did it on Tuesday, but I have to tell you I was in a terrible place, spiritually. I was up there singing my heart out to God while I saw everything in my life falling apart.

For the first time in our lives we had 100 percent sold out to God, with absolutely nothing held back. We were operating 100 percent on faith and nothing that we could see, taste, touch, hear or smell was telling us that God was going to honor our faith.

Then, on Wednesday morning, after I had sung my two songs, I went to my bride, Linda.

"You know, Honey, I just don't want to do this anymore. I must not have heard God right. Why don't we just pack it up and go back, because I just don't feel like doing this anymore,." I said.

My bride looked at me and said, "Glenn, you don't have to feel like doing anything. Faith has nothing to do with feeling." She said, "Just do it!"

You see, most people think I'm the one with faith. But that woman, my bride, Linda, is a faith-filled woman.

So I told her I needed to go outside and walk around and clear my head.

This retreat center covered two city blocks, and I'm walking around having this really intense conversation with God, with tears rolling down my face, and I remember saying, "Oh, Lord, you know the desire of my heart, you know I want to serve you and my church full-time. Would you please just show me a little something. It doesn't have to be a big deal, God, but show me that I didn't misunderstand what you were telling me."

So as I walked up the steps of this retreat center, I walked through the door and started walking toward the stage.

Now, keep in mind that there were a lot of people in this retreat center. As I'm walking toward the stage to begin my songs for the next program, this Catholic priest comes up to me. I didn't know who he was or where he was from. I hadn't seen him there the whole week.

He looked at me and said, "Glenn, this may sound a little strange, but about five minutes ago I was in the chapel, by myself, and while I was praying God said to me that I was to come to you and tell you that you have a powerful ministry. Then, I was supposed to invite you to my diocese and take you all over my diocese to let you preach and sing. Would you like to do that?"

I started to say, "Father, let me check my calendar to see if I have any openings."

You see, I had been in the corporate world too long.

What I did say was, "Father, you don't know what you just did for me. I'll get back to you and we'll work something out."

That was one of the most powerful moves of God in my life.

But, God wasn't through yet. Jesus knew I was going down for the third time.

As I started walking toward the stage, I glanced to my left and I saw this beautiful lady, she must have been about 70 years old. Well, as I was looking at this beautiful lady, she motioned for me to come over. I was preparing to go on stage for my next songs, so I almost told her I'd see her later.

But, you know, God made it very clear to me at that moment that I was supposed to go see her right then.

So, I walked over and she introduced herself and said, "Glenn, you probably don't remember me but on Monday morning, after you sang your first two songs, I asked you if you had a music CD or a music cassette."

At that time, of course, I didn't have anything like that. Then she said, almost in a hesitant voice, "Glenn, why don't you have a music CD or cassette?"

I said, "It costs over $5,000 to go into a recording studio and I don't even know where my next rent money will come from."

Then, this beautiful lady let out this groan. I could hear it clearly. The way it sounded I thought she was having a stroke.

"What's the problem?" I asked.

"Glenn," she said, "God woke me up on Monday morning, at 3 a.m. God never wakes me up! He told me I was supposed to give you the money to do that music recording. I've been fighting it for two days and I can't fight it anymore."

She took out her checkbook and she wrote me a check for $5,000, right on the spot. Then she handed me that check and said, "Glenn, go make that recording!"

That became our first music cassette, called "To God Be The Glory." I tell you, that recording has an anointing on it because God had His hand in the making of that tape.

That "free" Catholic Retreat Center conference paid me no money but God used that occasion to give me two of his most memorable and powerful moves of the Holy Spirit in my life.

In what areas of your life, right now, are you operating in faith, without any evidence that God is going to answer your need? Maybe it's a marriage that's falling apart, and you've been trying to save it and there's no evidence that it's going to be saved.

Stand on the promises of God!

Maybe it's a job, or the lack of a job. Maybe it's finances. Maybe it's your children, who are living a life that you just can't believe they're living and you've been praying and standing on faith.

Continue to stand on faith!

My brothers and sisters, whatever you're standing in faith on, right now at this very moment, if what you are praying for, if what you are hoping and believing in, is in line with the will of God, then it's going to happen. But it's going to happen in God's time and in God's way.

You see, we serve an "on time" God. God isn't early, God isn't late - although to us it often seems like God is late for our time schedule. But in God's way of thinking and acting, God is right on time.

Stand on the promises of Christ!

Believe that Jesus is really who He says He is!

Believe that His promises are true!

Believe that those promises are for you and for me!

You know, if I had to sum up this entire book with a particular Scripture, this would be the one. In your Bible, turn to the Gospel of John, Chapter 6, Verses 1-15. I first came across this Scripture over 30 years ago. I can't even begin to tell you how many hundreds of hours I have meditated, read, studied, reflected and prayed about this Scripture.

In 1983, I had the opportunity and distinct privilege of meeting Charlie Osborn of Pensacola, Florida. I believe that Charlie is truly one of the finest Catholic Lay Evangelists of all time. God used him as a powerful spiritual instrument to change the course of my life forever and I will always be grateful for his influence.

Charlie shared a commentary on the above mentioned Scripture and his words went to the core of my mind, heart and spirit. I remember weeping as I realized that I was in this Scripture.

Since that time, I have added my own thoughts and words, but I hope that you are as touched as I was and realize that you are also in this Scripture passage.

OK, Let's begin, "little boys and little girls."

"After this, Jesus went across to the other side of the Sea of Galilee. Jesus went up on the mountain and there He sat down. The Jewish feast of Passover was near..."

Now, it says in the Scripture that there were 5,000 people following Jesus. That's just the men. That does not include the women and children. There could have been as many as nine or 10 thousand people following and listening to Jesus Christ.

They weren't listening to Jesus in beautiful, carpeted, air-conditioned churches, and they weren't following Jesus in beautiful, air-conditioned cars or buses. They were sitting on the ground, they were wearing tunics. If they were fortunate enough, they had sandals on their feet. And they were walking up mountains and down valleys in all kinds of weather, all kinds of geography.

That tells me how powerful the message of Jesus was. These people could not get enough of Jesus Christ.

"When Jesus raised his eyes, He saw that a large crowd was following Him. So He turned to Philip, asking him where he could purchase enough food for the crowd to eat."

Now, Philip was one of the chosen ones. Jesus saw Philip every day, and Philip saw Jesus every day. Philip saw Jesus turn water into wine, he saw Jesus heal the blind, heal the deaf, heal the lame and raise Lazarus from the dead, but Philip still didn't get it.

Philip gives me a lot of hope.

"So, Jesus asked Philip where enough food could be bought to feed the crowd. He said this to test Philip, because He knew what He was going to do.

"Jesus, 200 days' wages for the food would not be enough for each one to have even a little bite," Philip replied.

I believe Philip was looking at Jesus and thinking, "Jesus, I know you raised Lazarus from the dead but even you can't pull this one off. Just tell them to go home."

Do you think Jesus was getting a little frustrated with Philip?

Don't you think Jesus just looked at Philip and said, "Philip, don't you get it? After all this time, don't you know who I am and don't you realize what I'm trying to do, to you, with you and through you?"

In this regard, nothing has changed in 2,000 years. I believe that everyday of our lives, Jesus looks at you and me and says, "Don't you get it? After all this time, don't you know who I am and don't you realize what I'm trying to do, to you, with you and through you?"

So often I don't get it. But my Lord Jesus - in His patience, love and mercy - just keeps gently asking the questions and offering me His grace.

"Then," according to Scripture, "Jesus turned to one of the other disciples, Andrew, the brother of Simon Peter." Andrew, again, was another of the chosen ones.

Andrew still didn't get it either but he had a little better grasp on this whole situation than Philip.

So, he turns to Jesus and says, "There's a boy here who has five barley loaves and some fish, but what good are those for so many?"

Jesus said, "Have the people recline."

I mentioned to you that I have been reflecting on this Scripture for almost 20 years. Have you ever wondered what happened from the moment when Andrew told Jesus there was a little boy with some food and when Jesus fed the entire crowd of probably far more than 10,000 men, women and children?

You see, Scripture doesn't say what happened in those moments before one of Jesus Christ's more memorable miracles.

I think that Jesus must have said something like this, "Andrew, will you go down there and ask that little boy to come to me?"

So Andrew walks down and he looks at this little guy and said, "Son, you know this man Jesus that you and the crowd have been following? He would very much like to see you."

And, I think that like any other little boy that age, I believe he probably looked at Andrew and said, "What does He want?"

So Andrew said to the little guy, "You see all these thousands of people? Well, they're hungry and you are the only one here who has any food."

That moment is where the rubber met the road for this little boy.

You see, he had two choices, the same two choices that we have today.

He could have looked at Andrew and said, "Andrew, go back and tell Jesus thanks, but no thanks."

Or, the boy could have gone behind a tree and consumed all of that food himself.

That was the choice I made the first 35 years of my life.

You see, as far as I was concerned, everything I had belonged to me. I was a self-made man. If you were hungry, that wasn't my problem. I hope you'll get some food but don't ask me. If you need a place to sleep, good luck. I hope you find it but don't ask me for help.

You see, at that time, everything I had - I consumed it all. Constantly.

Now the other choice was the one the little boy made.

He followed Andrew right back up to Jesus and when he got to Jesus, I think Jesus looked at him, turned him around and said, "You see all these people out there, these thousands of people? You think they're strangers, don't you? But, they're not. They're your brothers and sisters, they're your family and they're hungry. Will you give me that little bit of food you have in your hand and let me feed all of these people?"

I think that little boy looked at that food in his hand, looked at those thousands and thousands of people and then said, "Jesus, you can't be serious!"

Has Jesus ever asked you to do something and it seemed so impossible that you said, "Jesus, you can't be serious!"

In spite of his doubt, in spite of his confusion, this little boy looked at Jesus Christ and said, "Lord, I don't understand it, I don't get it, but if you can use me and what I have, here it is!"

And, that little boy gave Jesus everything he had. You see, that food was the boy's gifts and talents and he gave them to Jesus so He could multiply them. You all know what happened. Jesus fed everybody until they couldn't eat any more.

And then, as it says in that same Scripture, after everybody had eaten their fill they gathered everything remaining and there were 12 baskets of food left over. Then, I believe Jesus must have called this little boy over and said, "Son, you see all of this food? This is yours. Take it all home." Those 12 baskets of food were a blessing from God for that little boy.

You see, every day of our lives, Jesus wants to bless us with 12 basketfuls of blessings but so often He can't do it because we won't make the choice to be blessed.

I've discovered that, in that regard, nothing has changed in 2,000 years.

Today, Jesus is still looking for one little boy, or one little girl, who even in the midst of their doubts, their confusion, their fears will still say to Jesus, "Lord, if you can use me and what I have, my gifts and talents, I give them to you."

Over 20 years ago, Linda and I made the decision that we were going to be that little boy and that little girl, and in the midst of our tremendous doubts that Jesus would come through, that Jesus' promises were true and that Jesus was really who He said He was, we gave our Lord everything we had.

And, every day He blesses us with 12 basketfuls of blessings.

Will you be that little boy? Will you be that little girl?

Our world, and our Church, depends on you. It's all about commitment. It's all about serving one another.

I'd like to share this true story with you.

You see, God gives us so many true stories, so many opportunities with real life people and situations to share.

A number of years ago, Linda and I were giving a mission up in a small town in Louisiana. On Monday morning, the pastor, Father Peter, asked me if I would go visit a man in the hospital. All he would tell me is that it was a convalescent hospital and the man lived there. His name was John, he was 34 years old and he was a quadriplegic.

I asked the pastor how the man became a quadriplegic and found out that he was 17 years old when, on the night of his senior high school prom, he decided to drink and drive. He wrapped his car around a tree and for seventeen years he had been paralyzed from his neck on down.

So, at the hospital, I asked the nurse where he was. She pointed down a hallway and gave me a room number. When I got there, I stopped at the door and looked in. I saw a man in a motorized wheelchair.

He was facing two computer screens.

He didn't see me looking in, so I stood there momentarily and watched him.

Now the left computer screen had every letter in the alphabet on it and underneath the screen there was a long white tube that was attached to his mouth. There was a big screen on the right that was blank but there was a camera lens that came out from underneath the screen and it was aimed at his eyes.

Well, I watched John. He would bite down on that white tube in his mouth and somehow - they tried to explain it to me but I still couldn't understand it - he would move a letter from the left "alphabet" screen to the blank screen on the right with his eye motion.

When he would get the letter exactly where he wanted it on the right screen, he would release the pressure on the tube in his mouth and the letter would stay there. It took John several minutes to move four letters from the left screen to the right screen.

I must have coughed because John then realized there was somebody else in the room because he released his bite on the tube in his mouth and rolled over to me in his motorized wheelchair.

I introduced myself and said, "John, may I ask you what are you doing?"

He said he had a tube in his throat. Since he could only make a raspy sounding response, almost like a whisper, I had to get my ear right down next to the tube in his throat to hear him.

"I'm emailing people," he said.

"Well, John, who are you emailing?"

"Father Peter gives me the names of people who have left the Catholic church, so I email them and tell them that the church is less because they are not here and I invite them to come back home," John said.

I asked John how long it took him to write one email message.

"About four hours, Glenn," he replied.

"Why do you do this, John?" I asked him. "Nobody would fault you if you just lay in bed and complained all day long. You certainly have a lot to complain about."

He said, "Glenn, the only thing that matters to me in my life is that I am a good witness for the Lord."

As he spoke his next comment I just had to turn around and leave because I had started to cry.

"Glenn," John said, "I don't know what I would ever do if I lost my quality of life!"

When I walked out of that hospital and stood on the sidewalk, with tears still running down my cheeks, I began to think of all of the excuses that I used to use - and use even today - to not serve my God and my church.

When I hear God asking me to do something, when I see a need in my church that I know I can answer, I am still so quick to reach into my grab-bag of excuses and say, "Oh, Lord, I'm too busy. Oh, Lord, my back hurts too much."

But, that day on that sidewalk, I said, "Lord, if I'm ever about ready to tell you no, or I see a need in my church that I could serve and I'm about ready to say 'No,' please put John's face in my memory."

I have to tell you, since that day I met John, God has put John's face in my memory many times. When I think of John, with his second-by-second struggle just to get by and his determination to accomplish his emails for the Lord, I recall that all that mattered to John was that he was a good witness for the Lord.

You see, John finally understood what we all need to understand.

If you look at the crucifix in your Catholic church, or perhaps in your own home, and you see that commitment that our Lord Jesus Christ made for us, that's the commitment that John understood. And there was absolutely nothing that John was going to let get in the way of his returning that commitment to Jesus Christ.

My brothers and sisters, please take the lessons, insights and inspirations that hopefully you have received from reading this book, and begin living your life with a deeper commitment and a deeper love for Jesus Christ.

Find a place to connect with your church community. Take your gifts and talents and use them for the glory of God.

In the pages of this inspired book, God has planted spiritual seeds in your heart and God is going to bring those seeds to sprout, blossom and bear great fruit when He knows that the time is right for you.

Our Closing Prayer

Loving, gracious and merciful Father, we thank you from the bottom of our hearts for being with us each moment of each day, to help us become more aware of the areas that we need to change in our lives.

Lord, open our minds so that we can understand you in new ways.

Soften our hearts so that we can experience you in new ways.

We pray, Lord, that you will increase our desire and our faith to make a greater commitment to share your Gospel and the blessings and the riches of our Catholic Church.

May our Lord uplift you with His power, may He protect you with His love, may He return to you 30, 60 and 100 fold your generosity to Him in the ways that He knows you need His help and blessings the most.

May God bless you abundantly, and hold you in the palm of His hand.

We ask these things in the name of our precious Lord and Savior, Jesus Christ.

Amen.

A Call to Action

1. How do you see yourself walking with Jesus down the Road to Emmaus?

2. What questions are you asking Jesus as you walk with Him?

3. Are you willing to go back to your own Jerusalem, your family, your friends, neighbors, people you work with who may still be stuck at Calvary, and tell them you have seen the risen Christ?

4. What were your thoughts and feelings as you read the depiction of our Jesus's crucifixion.?

5. Knowing the commitment Jesus Christ made to you on the Cross, how might it challenge you to make a deeper, stronger commitment to Jesus Christ?

6. In what area of your life right now is God asking you to make a stronger commitment of your faith?

7. Will you be that "little boy" or "little girl" Jesus is looking for? How might that look in your life?

8. Is there anyone you are to share this book with? Pray about it.

CPSIA information can be obtained
at www.ICGtesting.com
Printed in the USA
FSOW02n1204021217
41662FS